In case of loss, please return

As a reward: £

Personal Information

Name

Surname

Home address

Phone number

E-mail

Work address

Work phone

Work e-mail

Western zodiac sign   Sun   Rising   Moon

Western zodiac element

Chinese zodiac sign

Chinese zodiac element

Dosha constitution

Birthstones

Affiliations / orders

Emergency contact

Affirmation for the year ahead

Resolution for daily practice

"True journey is return"
Ursula K. Le Guin

IGNOTA

Ignota Books is an experiment in the techniques of awakening. Founded in the last days of 2017 in the Peruvian mountains, Ignota publishes at the intersection of technology, myth-making and magic. Deriving our name from Hildegard of Bingen's mystical Lingua Ignota, we seek a language that makes possible the reimagining and re-enchantment of the world around us.

The Ignota Diary was born of the desire to create a tool for discovery. Intended as a companion and guide for charting our own journeys from one year to the next, our lessons and friendships form a part of the book you hold in your hands. We hope that it becomes of great use to you in the practice of everyday life.

ignota.org   @IgnotaBooks

Created and edited by **Sarah Shin** and **Ben Vickers**
Designed by **Cecilia Serafini**
Production edited by **Jay Drinkall**

Contributors
Acupressure by **Maria Christofi** Astrology by **SJ Anderson**
Ayurveda and Prajna by **Mira Manek** Dreamwork by **Jennifer Dumpert**
Herbal Remedies by **Paige Emery** Kriya Yoga by **Rachel Okimo**
Korean Ink Illustrations by **Jungran Kim** Mushroom Guide by **Ellen Percival**
Prayer Guide by **K Allado-McDowell** Regenerative Farming by **Elias Haase**
Rituals by **Pam Grossman** and **Himali Singh Soin** Ritual Spaces by **Leila Sadeghee**
Seed Bombs by **Jenna Sutela** Soji by **Shoukei Matsumoto**
Sonic Meditation by **Pauline Oliveros** Spellcraft by **Bones Tan-Jones**
Tarot by **CAConrad** and **T. Susan Chang** Weather by **Jay Drinkall**

Ignota © 2022
https://ignota.org/
http://crimson.vision

978-1-8380039-3-7

Birth Chart

Date of birth | Time
Place

Sun sign | Moon sign
Ascendant sign | Descendant sign

♈	Aries	♌	Leo	♐	Sagittarius
♉	Taurus	♍	Virgo	♑	Capricorn
♊	Gemini	♎	Libra	♒	Aquarius
♋	Cancer	♏	Scorpio	♓	Pisces

☽	Moon	♀	Venus	♄	Saturn	♇	Pluto	☋	South Node
☉	Sun	♂	Mars	♅	Uranus	⚷	Chiron	As	Ascendant
☿	Mercury	♃	Jupiter	♆	Neptune	☊	North Node	Mc	Midheaven

☌	Conjunction	✱	Sextile
☍	Opposition	∠	Semisquare
△	Trine	⚼	Sesquisquare
□	Square	⚻	Quincunx

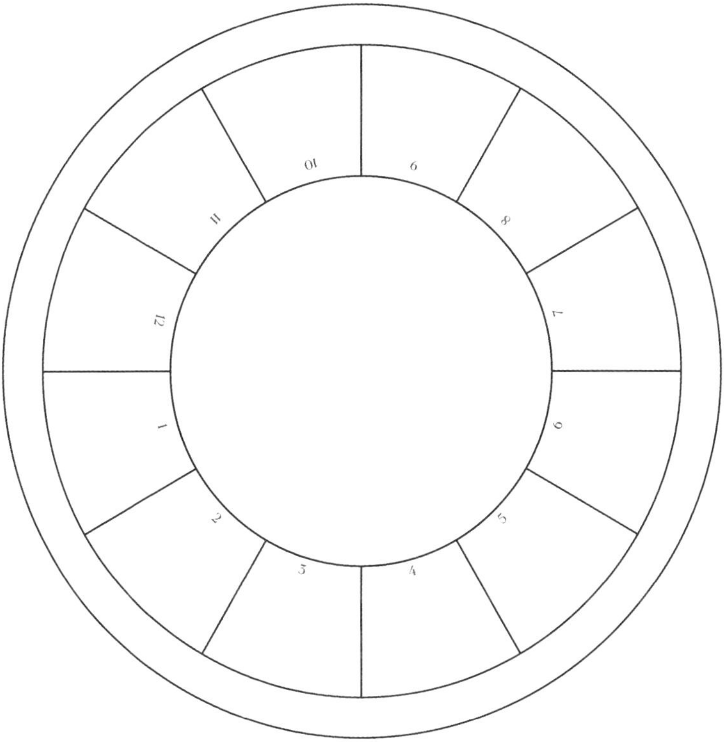

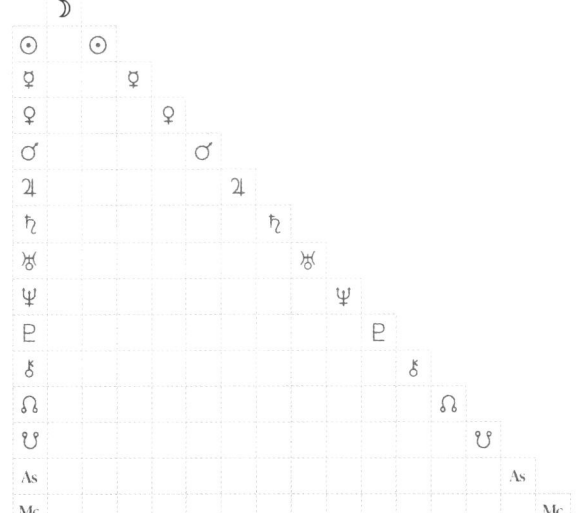

2023

January

	M	T	W	T	F	S	S
W52							1
W1	2	3	4	5	(6)	7	8
W2	9	10	11	12	13	14	15
W3	16	17	18	19	20	**21**	22
W4	23	24	25	26	27	28	29
W5	30	31					

February

	M	T	W	T	F	S	S
W5			1	2	3	4	(5)
W6	6	7	8	9	10	11	12
W7	13	14	15	16	17	18	19
W8	**20**	21	22	23	24	25	26
W9	27	28					

March

	M	T	W	T	F	S	S
W9			1	2	3	4	5
W10	6	(7)	8	9	10	11	12
W11	13	14	15	16	17	18	19
W12	20	**21**	22	23	24	25	26
W13	27	28	29	30	31		

April

	M	T	W	T	F	S	S
W13						1	2
W14	3	4	5	(6)	7	8	0
W15	10	11	12	13	14	15	16
W16	17	18	19	**20**	21	22	23
W17	24	25	26	27	28	29	30

May

	M	T	W	T	F	S	S
W18	1	2	3	4	(5)	6	7
W19	8	9	10	11	12	13	14
W20	15	16	17	18	**19**	20	21
W21	22	23	24	25	26	27	28
W22	29	30	31				

June

	M	T	W	T	F	S	S
W22				1	2	3	(4)
W23	5	6	7	8	9	10	11
W24	12	13	14	15	16	17	**18**
W25	19	20	21	22	23	24	25
W26	26	27	28	29	30		

Mercury Retrograde 2022

	Jan	Feb	Mar	Apr	May	Jun	Jul	Aug	Sep	Oct	Nov	Dec
Retrograde	▬▬▬			▬▬▬				▬▬▬				▬▬▬
	29.12 18/01			21.04 15.05				23.08 15/09				13.12 01/01

July

	M	T	W	T	F	S	S
W26					1	2	
W27	(3)	4	5	6	7	8	9
W28	10	11	12	13	14	15	16
W29	●17	18	19	20	21	22	23
W30	24	25	26	27	28	29	30
W31	31						

August

	M	T	W	T	F	S	S
W31		(1)	2	3	4	5	6
W32	7	8	9	10	11	12	13
W33	14	15	●16	17	18	19	20
W34	21	22	23	24	25	26	27
W35	28	29	30	(31)			

September

	M	T	W	T	F	S	S
W35					1	2	3
W36	4	5	6	7	8	9	10
W37	11	12	13	14	●15	16	17
W38	18	19	20	21	22	23	24
W39	25	26	27	28	(29)	30	

October

	M	T	W	T	F	S	S
W39							1
W40	2	3	4	5	6	7	8
W41	9	10	11	12	13	●14	15
W42	16	17	18	19	20	21	22
W43	23	24	25	26	27	(28)	29
W44	30	31					

November

	M	T	W	T	F	S	S
W44			1	2	3	4	5
W45	6	7	8	9	10	11	12
W46	●13	14	15	16	17	18	19
W47	20	21	22	23	24	25	26
W48	(27)	28	29	30			

December

	M	T	W	T	F	S	S
W48					1	2	3
W49	4	5	6	7	8	9	10
W50	11	●12	13	14	15	16	17
W51	18	19	20	21	22	23	24
W52	25	26	(27)	28	29	30	31

● **New Moon** Best for starting projects, writing intentions and planting seeds. A potent time to call things into being.

○ **Full Moon** Peak lunar energy enabling purging, illumination and reveals (but not necessarily the full picture). Practice rituals and spells to burn, release or purify and charge crystals and magical tools under the moonlight.

2024

January

	M	T	W	T	F	S	S
W1	1	2	3	4	5	6	7
W2	8	9	10	11	12	13	14
W3	15	16	17	18	19	20	21
W4	22	23	24	25	26	27	28
W5	29	30	31				

February

	M	T	W	T	F	S	S
W5				1	2	3	4
W6	5	6	7	8	9	10	11
W7	12	13	14	15	16	17	18
W8	19	20	21	22	23	24	25
W9	26	27	28	29			

March

	M	T	W	T	F	S	S
W9					1	2	3
W10	4	5	6	7	8	9	10
W11	11	12	13	14	15	16	17
W12	18	19	20	21	22	23	24
W13	25	26	27	28	29	30	31

April

	M	T	W	T	F	S	S
W14	1	2	3	4	5	6	7
W15	8	9	10	11	12	13	14
W16	15	16	17	18	19	20	21
W17	22	23	24	25	26	27	28
W18	29	30					

May

	M	T	W	T	F	S	S
W18			1	2	3	4	5
W19	6	7	8	9	10	11	12
W20	13	14	15	16	17	18	19
W21	20	21	22	23	24	25	26
W22	27	28	29	30	31		

June

	M	T	W	T	F	S	S
W22						1	2
W23	3	4	5	6	7	8	9
W24	10	11	12	13	14	15	16
W25	17	18	19	20	21	22	23
W26	24	25	26	27	28	29	30

July

	M	T	W	T	F	S	S
W27	1	2	3	4	5	6	7
W28	8	9	10	11	12	13	14
W29	15	16	17	18	19	20	21
W30	22	23	24	25	26	27	28
W31	29	30	31				

August

	M	T	W	T	F	S	S
W31				1	2	3	4
W32	5	6	7	8	9	10	11
W33	12	13	14	15	16	17	18
W34	19	20	21	22	23	24	25
W35	26	27	28	29	30	31	

September

	M	T	W	T	F	S	S
W35							1
W36	2	3	4	5	6	7	8
W37	9	10	11	12	13	14	15
W38	16	17	18	19	20	21	22
W39	23	24	25	26	27	28	29
W40	30						

October

	M	T	W	T	F	S	S
W40		1	2	3	4	5	6
W41	7	8	9	10	11	12	13
W42	14	15	16	17	18	19	20
W43	21	22	23	24	25	26	27
W44	28	29	30	31			

November

	M	T	W	T	F	S	S
W44					1	2	3
W45		5	6	7	8	9	10
W46		12	13	14	15	16	17
W47		19	20	21	22	23	24
W48		26	27	28	29	30	

December

	M	T	W	T	F	S	S
W48							1
W49	2	3	4	5	6	7	8
W50	9	10	11	12	13	14	15
W51	16	17	18	19	20	21	22
W52	23	24	25	26	27	28	29
	30	31					

Daily Practice

"Your task is not to seek for love, but merely to seek and find all the barriers within yourself that you have built against it."
—Jalāl ad-Dīn Muhammad Rūmī

The establishment of daily practice, a devotional rhythm in life through ritual and routine can have transformative effects on your consciousness, health and general well-being.

The focus and nature of one's personal path can create significant differences in the range and structure of a daily practice. It's important to construct a series of rituals that make sense to you, complement one another and can be built on easily over time. As this process of self-realisation begins to unfold, guiding you inward, you may experience a shift in the way you perceive the world and its challenges.

"You have the right to work, but never to the fruit of work. You should never engage in action for the sake of reward, nor should you long for inaction. Perform work in this world, Arjuna, as a man established within himself – without selfish attachments, and alike in success and defeat."
—The Bhagavad Gita

Fundamentals of Basic Daily Practice

Tracking progression: as transformation is incremental and subtle, a journal is helpful to reflect upon your gradual development.
Consistency and discipline: a daily practice can seem difficult to maintain in contemporary life. The key is to start with a simple commitment and stick to it. Rather than attempting to begin with an hour of meditation each day and failing, start by aiming to meditate for five minutes.
Sadhana: the Sanskrit word Sadhana means "conscious spiritual practice". Unlike a fitness routine, deepening your practice involves a dedication to learning and spiritual growth. The intention and actions you set out in the world should be about more than individual gain, and attend to the relationship that you bear to the collective.

There are many different traditions that can provide a starting point for a daily practice. The following two examples suggest how one can weave a practice into the fabric of everyday life. Knowing where to start can be challenging, but selecting two or three of these individual actions every day can provide a good foundation for further development.

Daily Yogic Practice

Morning Asana (20-30 minutes): adopt a morning *asana* (physical postures or movements) sequence from a chosen school of yoga to repeat each morning.
Pranayama (5-10 minutes): cultivating breath control to access the subtler dimensions of *prana* (life-force) has many benefits, including pacifying the nervous system. Samavritti Pranayama is a good place to start, but consider what your own body and mind need and adjust accordingly.
Morning Meditation (20 minutes): there are many methods and aids to meditation, such as focussing on a mantra or observing the breath. You may use mala beads to help you count mantras. There is no such thing as good or bad meditation: the most important thing is to start and to sit down everyday.
Sacred Ritual (5-10 minutes): ending your seated meditation by creating a space to set your intentions for the day ahead and to honour the sense of something greater than yourself is very powerful. Make a loving offering of flowers, food, water or light to honour the divine, or follow a practice of attunement to the qualities represented by the four cardinal directions.
Blessing Food: Ayurveda teaches that how we eat is as important as what we eat. Take a moment before eating to give thanks and bless your food. You may hold your hands with the palms facing down above your food, bringing your awareness to the energetic connection between the meal and your breath.
Evening Meditation (20 minutes): before rest, settle the mind with an evening session of meditation.
Gratitude: cultivate gratitude, stillness, surrender and love – the path of devotional or Bhakti yoga – as the final act of your day. Practice a short heart-opening asana sequence, or chant a devotional mantra, or take a seat with your hands in Anjali Mudra (bring your hands to prayer position at the heart center and lightly press your thumbs into the sternum) and allow gratitude to arise within you.

Daily Magical Practice

Opening Magical Space: before and after meditation utilise the invocation and banishment rituals of the pentagram and hexagram as described by the Hermetic Order of the Golden Dawn.

Morning Meditation (20 minutes): meditation is the first practice one should undertake, because without concentration and stillness of thought, there is no magic.

Daily Tarot: following meditation, with eyes half-closed, draw a single card from the deck to guide your day.

Offerings: at your altar, light a candle and make a simple offering with a cup of water to the deities or spirits from which you seek guidance and power.

Book of Shadows: before breakfast, make time for reflection in your journal.

Contemplation: during the day, take a moment to pause in silence and observe the natural environment around you, whether appreciating the sun or walking in a park or forest.

Study (1 hour): serious dedication to practice requires regular study of a range of subjects.

Prayer: at the end of each day, return to your altar and dedicate your energy to those deities you have committed to serve.

Daily Practice

Take time at the beginning of your year to structure a daily practice, making sure to check in and make modifications to your practice throughout the year.

Morning

Day

Night

Monthly Review

January

February

March

April

May

June

July

August

September

October

November

December

1 Eibingen Abbey
49°59'33''N 7°55'41''E
Founded by mystic and saint Hildegard of Bingen.

2 Göbekli Tepe
37°13'23''N 38°55'21''E
Ritual site built by hunter gatherers during the 8th millennium BCE.

3 Whanganui River
39°56.89'S 174°59.22'E
Sacred to the Māori people, the first river to be granted legal person status.

4 Bodh Gaya
24.695102°N 84.991275°E
The holy site of Gautama Buddha's enlightenment.

5 Urubamba River
10°42'07''S 73°45'15''W
Earthly counterpart to the dark constellations of the Inca Milky Way.

6 Ancient Library of Alexandria
31°12'N 29°55'E
Great storehouse of knowledge, now lost in time.

7 Obelisk of Axum
14°7'55.8''N 38°43'10.8''E
Stelae erected during the 4th century CE by the Kingdom of Aksum.

8 Rishikesh
30°05'16.1"N 78°16'09.3"E
Gateway to the Garhwal Himalayas, yoga capital of the world.

9 Damanhur
45.416915°N 7.747598°E
Extensive underground site for the Temples of Humankind, built in 1978.

10 Mount Shasta
41°25'26.1"N 122°11'48.3"W
True home of the Lemurians.

11 Emma Kunz Grotto
47°26'54.8"N 8°21'24.1"E
Home of the miraculous healing rock AION-A.

12 Yakushima Island
30°20'38''N 130°31'26''E
An ancient and sacred forest.

The Astrology of 2023: Excavations in the Age of Air
by SJ Anderson

A new Age of Air kicked off on the winter solstice in 2020, with Jupiter and Saturn conjoining in the first degree of Aquarius. The element of air is intangible; it's felt but not seen. In the same way that magic alters reality to meet the indomitable human will, technology and innovation – propelled by the element of air – manifest phenomena once thought impossible.

The astrology of 2023 builds upon this shift into a new epoch of high fascination. Pluto, the planet of the underworld, carries an oversized force. Pluto unearths the things we're unaware of, but that still operate unseen. 2023 sees this powerful dwarf planet spend the first two-and-a-half months of its long, twenty-one-year dredge through Aquarius. All of Pluto's time in Aquarius this year will be in the first degree, including its retrograde station on May Day. This preview and punctuation – 23 March through 11 June – provides a window into what's to come, functioning as both looking glass and accelerant.

The extreme shifts during the first years of the 2020s came on with such speed that Pluto's time in Aquarius may be one of our first chances to stop and look at what we've become. We're gazing through the depths and breaching the other side – experiencing that which formerly existed only in rumour. Consistent and ongoing revolutions in digital and biological fields over the last forty years are now brought to the fore, cueing a robust collision with past ways of living: human bodies are seen as vast mines, with biological life digitally interconnected as never before. The perilous task of doing what one wills, nobly and held in love, has the highest stakes yet. The potential rewards are huge, and so are the dangers. And yet, paradoxically, 2023 also sees an abandonment of Aquarian ambition.

On 7 March Saturn enters the healing waves of Pisces, marking the completion of six years of gaining immense force during its run through Capricorn and Aquarius. Saturn will not return to its zodiacal homes until 2047–53. Instead of tightening controls in the face of uncertainty, we're learning to release into the promise of a more evolved tomorrow. As futuristic visions begin to flower, the divine elegance of the illogical – the tumult inherent to the nature of time – asks that we embrace new experiences without timidity.

The Planets Through the Months

January begins with Mars in Gemini and Mercury in Capricorn, both retrograde. Mars' long stint in Mercury-ruled Gemini, since August 2022, has settled the force of intellect into a place of weariness. Word fatigue and jumbled cognition fade after Mars' (12 January) and Mercury's (18 January) direct stations, which ramp up the second half of January and energise the young year. Saturn in Aquarius perfects the final of its three sextiles with dwarf planet Eris in Aries on 15 January. The lawless, chaotic side of new societal norms help to assuage the discomfort of their implementation. Jupiter – back in its power degrees in early Aries since late December 2022 – adds to a synergy of empowerment: Mars' renewed movement forward in Gemini teams up with Jupiter via a free-flowing sextile. On 27 January, Venus enters Pisces, the sign of its exaltation, bringing felicity and ornamentation to the final week of January. The Sun's yearly purification of Saturn via a conjunction happens in Aquarius on 16 February, giving Saturn a final opportunity to complete the installation of its novel regimes of order and sterility. Saturn leaves Aquarius for good to enter Pisces on 7 March, where its rigid enforcement is washed with great waves of cleansing alterations.

March is a key month of the year. The ingress of the Sun into Aries on 20 March occurs while Venus is in Taurus. This, plus Mars in Gemini being mutually received by Mercury in Aries, adds to the tenor of the astrological year (March 2023 – March 2024), which is led by flavours of homemade artisanship and incisive phraseology. Saturn's departure from Aquarius (7 March) occurs two weeks before Pluto enters Aquarius (23 March). We trade Saturn's regulation and correction for Pluto's single-pointed density. The texture, make up and stability of the rules Saturn has imposed over the last few years now come under Pluto's inspection. It's an arduous and complex task that gives context to the rise of biotechnology and digital omnipresence. The expanding, avatar-based metaverse and the tokenised, transactional 'Web3' become more strongly integrated into everyday life.

Mars' entry into Cancer (25 March) brings long-awaited relief. After eight months in Gemini, Mars is allowed much-needed rest. Cancer, the caretaker of the zodiac, asks Mars to set aside its craving for breakage and instead defer to more sustainable methods. April brings a truth warrior mentality when the Sun conjoins Jupiter in Aries (11 April): it's less a 'take no prisoners' philosophy and more an impulse to protect those near and dear. A solar eclipse in Aries (20 April) swiftly follows, bringing about change through tampered down, introspective methods. In Cancer, Mars must restrain its vigour; its impetus to run free must find more settled, domestic outlets. Between eclipses, a period of disarray may ensue when Mercury stations retrograde in Taurus (21 April) and Jupiter conjoins Eris, the dwarf planet of dissension, in Aries

(24 April). The lunar eclipse in Scorpio (5 May) makes it more important than ever to channel frustration, as both spring eclipses are ruled by Mars in its detriment in Cancer. A commitment to service and to nurturing dependents is essential, even in the face of unanticipated predicaments.

Mercury stations direct in Taurus (15 May) – Venus' earth domicile, the sign of the Bull – the day before Jupiter enters the same sign (16 May). All of Mercury's retrogrades in 2023 begin and end in earth signs, suggesting that considering the physical, tangible environment will become even more crucial as the Age of Air beckons us further toward screens and ethereal perceptions. Jupiter in Taurus makes for a satisfying arrival, coming just as the North Node's long stay in the same sign nears completion. And Jupiter in Taurus escalates fast. First, this planet of truth, hope, and abundance squares Pluto (18 May), giving Pluto's initial months in Aquarius an initiatory lift. Intensifying this wrestle between fixed signs, Mars in Leo then squares Jupiter (23 May), igniting even more fireworks. Subsequently, Jupiter conjoins the North Node (2 June), initiating potentially unstable appetites for delicacy, eroticism and kinship.

There's a return to the more Saturnine times of the beginning of the decade when Pluto retrogrades back into Capricorn (11 June) days before Saturn stations retrograde in Pisces (17 June). Jupiter's sextile with Saturn comes immediately thereafter (19 June). Saturn's changing frameworks in Pisces make for unfamiliar territory, but past revelations can serve as pathways through this new ground, especially with the support of Jupiter. When the North Node and South Node enter Aries and Libra respectively (17 July), our approach to relating assumes a more determined posture.

After two years of eclipses in Taurus and Scorpio, 2023 is a transition year. The remaining two eclipses (of four) now occur in the Aries-Libra axis but are new in sign only, as Mars and Venus will remain planetary rulers of eclipses until late 2024. The question 'What does it mean to love well?' is reconfigured into: 'What practices can be implemented to embrace a newfound awareness of the force of love?'

Mars in Virgo opposes Saturn in Pisces on 20 July, hurling us into overwhelm, days before Venus' sesquiennial renewal, which begins with its retrograde station in Leo (23 July). The rush of others' offered delights, though enticing, is best considered through a lens of delayed gratification. That same day, Pluto in Capricorn conjoins the South Bending (23 July), squaring the lunar nodes. The work of unearthing proceeds with another plunge into themes of the Pluto in Capricorn years (2008–24), a period of radical technological connectivity and continuous economic upheaval. Venus conjoining the Sun in Leo on 13 August seeds a new synodic cycle for the planet of touch and colour. What better way to explore selfhood and consciousness than through the senses? Bringing sexuality into spiritual practice is one path for engaging with Venus' rebirth in Leo.

Late summer sees a flurry of planetary stations: Mercury stations retrograde in Virgo (23 August) and goes direct there three weeks later (15 September), providing a pause from intellectual predominance ideal for anticipating the fall months; Venus stations direct in Leo (4 September), kicking off a renewal of vows with those we love; and Jupiter stations retrograde (4 September), supporting a step back from the intensity of the multicoloured bursts of Jupiter's first months in Taurus.

October brings two eclipses ruled by Venus under Virgo's scrutiny, the pair beckoning us further into the nuances of gratification and generation. A solar eclipse on 14 October, the first to occur in Libra since March 2016, highlights intentionality and deliberation in how we relate to others. A lunar eclipse in Taurus follows on 28 October, accentuating creative acts such as painting: there may be inversions within the normal flow of comfort and breakthroughs in how one approaches a canvas.

Saturn's direct station in Pisces (4 November) reopens the spigots. Piscean storms of change blow through the final months of the year, their waters hurled towards a final, natural settlement. Mars is reborn in Scorpio on 18 November, an opportune time to enact long-planned strategies derived from fiercely held motivations. This conjunction prepares Mars – which has just entered Sagittarius – to square off with Saturn (25 November). Metamorphosis requires breaking through the limitations of the status quo. Whirlwinds continue when Eris conjoins the North Node in Aries (27 November), ignoring imposed structure in service of higher, less tangible ways of ordering.

The year closes with Mercury stationing retrograde in Capricorn (13 December) before entering Sagittarius (23 December). Pausing games of business and mind provides space for the celebration of the winter solstice. Jupiter stations direct in Taurus in the early morning on New Year's Eve, certifying that the party ushering in 2024 will be luscious, raunchy and full of joy.

Astrological Houses

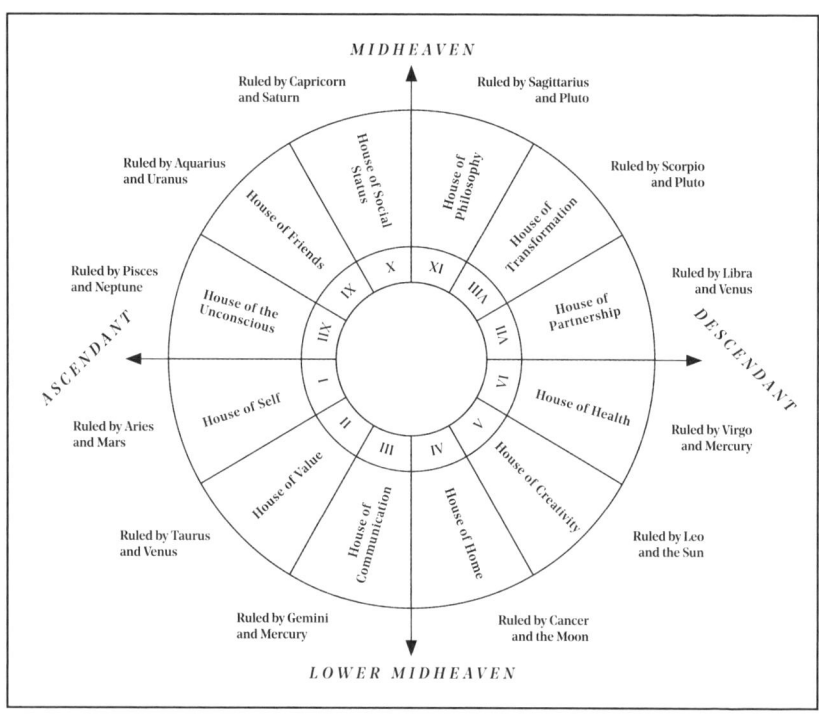

1st, of Self: identity, beginnings, how you appear to others, physical traits, approach to life. Cusp is the Ascendent or Rising sign.

2nd, of Value: money, security, possessions, feelings around material stability, finances, self-worth.

3rd, of Communication: everyday communication with immediate family and community, apprenticeship, early education.

4th, of Home: domestic life, emotions, roots, relationship with parents, foundations. Cusp is the Imum Coeli (IC).

5th, of Creativity: romance, love, pleasure, play, children, fertility, self-expression, invention, drama, attitude towards fun.

6th, of Health: service, job or employment by someone else, work habits, fitness, hygiene, organisation, discipline, daily routine, responsibilities.

7th, of Partnership: relationships, business and personal partnerships, marriage, sharing, joint endeavours, interpersonal style. Cusp is the Descendant.

8th, of Transformation: sex, death, intimacy, regeneration, magic, other people's resources and money, legacies, wills, taxes.

9th, of Philosophy: higher learning, travel, publishing, wisdom, ethics, religious and mystical patterns, cross-cultural relations, luck.

10th, of Social Status: reputation, career, authority, achievement, awards, boundaries, rules. Cusp is Midheaven or Medium Coeli (MC).

11th, of Friends: community, collective endeavour, humanitarianism, good fortune, benefactors, innovation, technology, hopes, wishes for the future.

12th, of the Unconscious: karma, endings, healing, solitude, hidden resources, hidden problems, social responsibility.

PLANETARY BODIES

Sun: Ruler of Leo, 5th house of creativity. Ego, identity and purpose. Pride, warmth, heart, vitality, illumination, strength. Will, recognition and our future goals.

Moon: Ruler of Cancer, 4th house of home. Emotions, the unconscious and responses. Female principle (yin) – mother, wife, daughter. Accommodation, retreat, habits, food, nurturing.

PLANETS

Mercury: Ruler of Gemini and Virgo, 3rd house of communication and 6th house of health. Thought, speech, writing. Connections, the rational mind and opinions. School and learning. Service, job or employment. Habits, organisation, hygiene. Siblings.

Venus: Ruler of Taurus and Libra, 2nd house of value and 7th house of partnership. Love, harmony, happiness. Giving, sharing and compromise. Art, beauty, taste. Comparison, means of exchange, money.

Mars: Ruler of Aries, 1st house of self. Identity, beginnings. Action, assertion and appearances. Resourcefulness, survival, courage. Endurance and fight.

Jupiter: Ruler of Sagittarius, 9th house of philosophy. Vision, faith, confidence, beliefs of all kinds. Wisdom, wealth and meaning. Travel, expansion and exaggeration.

Saturn: Ruler of Capricorn, 10th house of social status. Authority, discipline, duties, responsibilities. Fear, control and denial. Defences. Perseverance and tenacity.

Uranus: Ruler of Aquarius, 11th house of friends. Community and collective. Innovation and technology. Liberation, revolution and rebellion. Dynamic, adaptable, unpredictable.

Neptune: Ruler of Pisces, 12th house of the unconscious. Refinement, purification and cleansing. Enchantment, deception, fantasies. Transcendence or escape. Sensitivity, ideals, dreams. Sacrifice.

Pluto: Ruler of Scorpio, 8th house of transformation and change. Sex, death, intimacy, regeneration and rebirth. Obsession, paranoia and compulsion. Taboo. Crisis and survival.

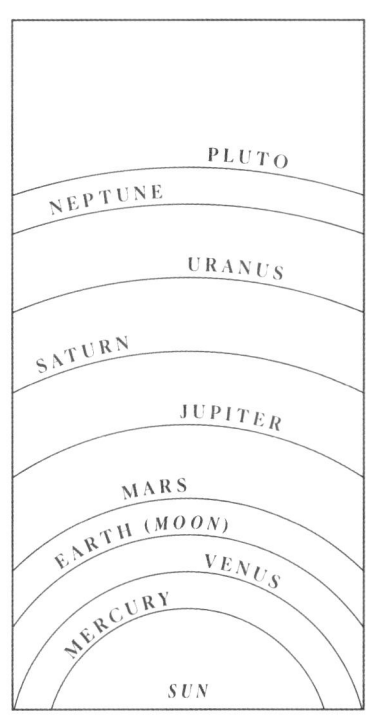

ASTEROIDS

Lilith: The dark side. Refusal, non-submittal, non-compromise. Standing up to power dynamics. Collective anger and rage. Feminine rage associated with patriarchal suppression.

Chiron: The wounded healer. Hard work. Self-reflection. Healing.

Ceres: The nurturer. Food, cooking, nutrition and gardening.

Pallas: Creative intellect, the weaver of patterns. Wisdom and intuition. Healing. Sculpture, pottery and medicinal properties.

Juno: Intimate relationships, partnership. Boundaries. Sharing. Bitterness and jealousy. Authority and control. Femininity, conception and pregnancy.

Vesta: Self-sufficiency. Commitment to women and sisterhood. Service to the goddess. Wholeness and purity.

Moon Phases

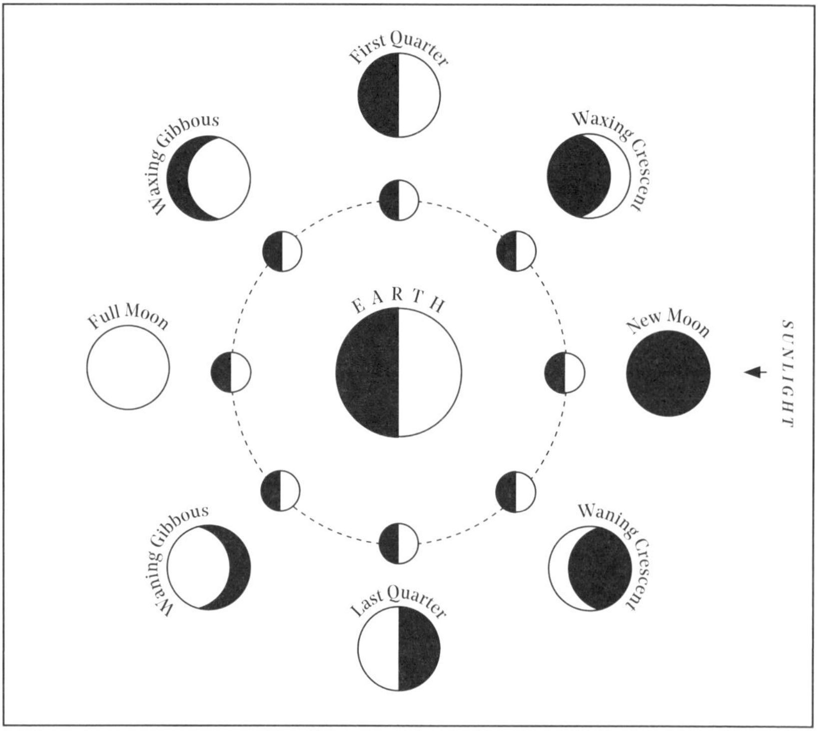

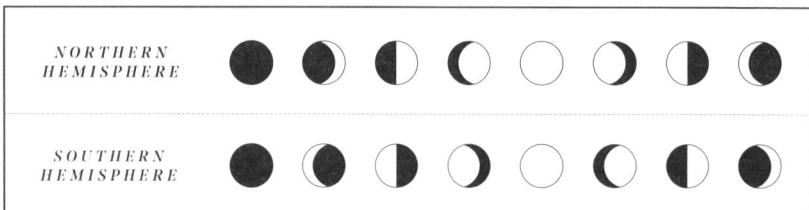

New Moon: Best for starting projects, writing intentions and planting seeds. A potent time to call things into being.

First Quarter Moon: A good time for gathering information, making new connections, building energy. Work with this lunar energy to enhance, commit and expand.

Full Moon: Peak lunar energy enabling purging, illumination and reveals (but not necessarily the full picture). Practice rituals and spells to burn, release or purify and charge crystals and magical tools under the moonlight.

Last Quarter Moon: A time for self-reflection, restorative self-care, dreamwork and letting go. Tarot or between-the-worlds communication are served well by this energy.

It is best not to practice moon magic during eclipses.

Weekly Planner

New Moon ●
First Quarter ◐
Full Moon ○
Last Quarter ◑

Data given in Coordinated Universal Time (UTC)

December
January

Week 52

Monday
26

Tuesday
27

Wednesday
28

Thursday
29

Friday
30

1 January Hatsumode or hatsumairi (Japan), the Shinto holy day marking a new year. Early in the morning, visit shrines to thank the *kami* (spirits), request good fortune and make resolutions for the year ahead.

1 January 1977 The Minoan Brotherhood is founded in Eddie Buczynski's New York flat. Dissatisfied with LGBT exclusion in Gardnerian Wicca, the Brotherhood aims to be 'a mystery/initiatory cult which erotically celebrates Life through male love'.

1 January 1889 During the total solar eclipse over Western America, the Paiute healer Wovoka receives a vision prophesying the return of the dead, the exodus of white colonisers from North America and an age of unity and prosperity for Native American peoples. The practice of the Ghost Dance, which hastens the fulfillment of the prophecy, spreads to much of the Western United States.

Early January A good time to sow basil (*ocimum basilicum*) for an early crop in May. In European lore, basil is Satan's herb, requiring cursed ground to grow properly, hence the French idiom for ranting, *'semer le basilic'* ('to sow the basil'). A fragrant and versatile culinary herb, basil is associated with Mars and Scorpio, and has a wide range of magical properties. Use in exorcisms and protection spells, as well as to attract money, luck and love.

Notes

Saturday
31

Sunday
1

January

Week 1

Monday
2

Tuesday
3

Wednesday
4

Thursday
5

Friday
6

in Cancer

4 January 2008 Death of John O'Donohue, Irish poet, author, priest and Hegelian philosopher, best known for re-popularising neo-Celtic spirituality. 'Thoughts are our inner senses. Infused with silence and solitude, they bring out the mystery of inner landscape.'

5 January 2023 Birthday of Guru Gobind Singh in 1666. Guru Gobind Singh introduced many of the customs that Sikhs practise today, including the five Ks: the Kesh (uncut hair), Kangha (wooden comb), Kara (iron bracelet), Kachera (cotton underwear) and Kirpan (iron dagger).

5 January Twelfth Night, the last night of the Twelve Days of Christmas. To leave Christmas decorations hanging after this date is considered unlucky, perhaps due to an old belief in tree-spirits living in the winter greenery traditionally used as Christmas decorations. Brought into the house to provide a safe haven for the tree spirits during winter, they must be released back into the countryside in order for spring to return.

7 January 1891 Zora Neale Hurston, writer, folklorist, anthropologist and ethnographer, is born in Notasulga, Alabama. The first African American woman to be trained as an anthropologist, she found in Vodou a crucible for transformation. Her novel *Their Eyes Were Watching God* is written in Haiti on a research trip into the region's folk and magical-spiritual culture. 'Gods always behave like the people who make them.'

7–9 January 2023 Mahāyāna New Year, a Buddhist celebration falling on the first sighting of the full moon in January. Celebrate by honouring and praying to the gods, particularly Buddha, bathing his statues as a show of respect. Light candles as offerings to ensure happiness for the coming year.

Notes

Saturday
7

Sunday
8

January

Week 2

Monday
9

Tuesday
10

Wednesday
11   Eris stations direct

Thursday
12   Mars stations direct

Friday
13

10 January 1998 The first official Fête du Vodoun (Benin), a national holiday celebrating Vodou as a religion and heritage. Thousands of people from around the world gather in the city of Ouidah to receive blessings from the *roi*, Daagbo Hounon Houna II, and partake in gin, dancing, sacrifice, singing and possession.

10 January 2004 *Caliban and the Witch: Women, the Body and Primitive Accumulation* by Silvia Federici is published. A hugely influential feminist text mapping the history of the body, it argues that the witch-hunts of the sixteenth and seventeenth centuries were tools to discipline and control women.

13 January Nuutinpäivä (Finland), a celebration where young men dress as goats by wearing inverted fur jackets, birch masks and horns. They wander from house to house, blundering in to demand food and alcohol. Likely connected with the fact that in the old calendar it was New Year's Eve. In Ukraine and Belarus a similar parade of revellers visits houses, playing pranks, guided by a bachelor in women's clothes driving a goat.

13 January Saint Hilary's Day. The son of pagans and father of Saint Abra, during the fourth century Saint Hilary was Bishop of Poitiers, France. According to tradition, 'Saint Hilary's is the coldest day of the year.'

15 January 2023 Makar Sankranti, Hindu midwinter celebration marking the transition of the sun from Sagittarius to Capricorn. Celebrations vary by region and can involve the flying of kites, attendance of fairs, worship of the Sun God and submergence, to purify the self and bestow *punya* or virtue.

Notes

Saturday
14

Sunday
15

☽ in Libra
Saturn sextile Eris

January

Week 3

Monday
16

Tuesday
17

Wednesday
18

Mercury stations direct

Thursday
19

Friday
20

20 January 1879 Georgy Chulkov, poet and critic, is born in Moscow, Russia. With Vyacheslav Ivanov, Chulkov becomes a proponent of Mystical Anarchism, a mixture of theosophy, occultism, symbolist and decadent poetry and the Joachimite idea of a Third Revelation.

21 January Babinden (Bulgaria), a traditional feast to celebrate midwives. All women who gave birth the previous year bring their babies to the midwife's house to be anointed with honey and butter. After feasting and drinking, the tipsy women prank men who must pay money to be left alone.

22 January 2018 Death of Ursula K. Le Guin, myth-maker, feminist and voyager, aged 88 in Portland, Oregon. 'Magic exists in most societies in one way or another, and one of the forms it exists in a lot of places is, if you know a thing's true name, you have power over the thing, or the person.'

21 January 2023 Bituun (Mongolia), the day before the feasting of Tsagaan Sar, the Mongolian new year. Today, during the dark moon period, clean homes and barns thoroughly. Light candles and leave three pieces of ice at the doorway for Palden Lhamo's horse to drink; she is visiting every house tonight. Settle issues and pay debts, then meet your family and await the new year.

22 January 2023 Lunar New Year, celebrated in China, the Republic of Korea, Mongolia, Tibet and Vietnam. The year of the Water Rabbit is the fourth in the twelve-year rotation cycle of the Chinese zodiac.

Notes

Saturday
21

● in Aquarius

Sunday
22

Uranus stations direct

January

Week 4

Monday
23

Tuesday
24

Wednesday
25

Thursday
26

Friday
27

23 January 1967 Birth of Belkis Ayón, artist and printmaker, in Havana, Cuba. Best known for her collographs based on Abakuá, a secret Afro-Cuban society that began in Nigeria and was brought to Haiti and Cuba in the nineteenth century through the slave trade.

Early 1947 Death of Stephany Robinson, South Carolina root worker and practitioner of West African-derived folk medicine and magic. The original 'Dr. Buzzard', renowned for his healings and ritual work, is said to have inherited his powers from his father, who had been brought from West Africa despite the antebellum ban on the importation of enslaved people from Africa. He is well-known for the practice of 'chewing the root' in court, so that the defendants would be let loose or given a light sentence.

25 January 1759 Robert Burns, Scotland's *de facto* national poet, is born in Alloway, Scotland. A tenant farmer during the economic shift from agriculture to industry during the Industrial Revolution, Burns's poems often express a deep, spiritual reverence of nature, and the pain of seeing ways of life connected to its rhythms pass into obsolescence. 'Yet nature's charms, the hills and woods, / The sweeping vales, and foaming floods, / Are free alike to all.'

25 January St Dwynwen's Day (Wales). The patron saint of friendship and love, Dwynwen is believed to have been a daughter of the legendary King Brychan Brycheiniog during the fifth century.

Notes

Saturday
28

☾ in Taurus

Sunday
29

January
February

Week 5

Monday
30

Tuesday
31

Wednesday
1

Thursday
2

Friday
3

Ceres stations retrograde

30 January 2023 Sadeh (Iran), an ancient Zoroastrian festival dating back to the Achaemenid empire, also known as Adur-Jashan (Feast of Fire). Pray and dance around the bonfire, banishing cold and darkness. Let the fire burn all night, and in the morning take a small portion to the hearth of your home.

31 January 1942 Derek Jarman, filmmaker, writer, artist, gardener and gay rights activist, is born Michael Derek Elworthy Jarman in London. A cinematic alchemist, Jarman's interest in Renaissance occult philosophy, prompted by his readings of Jung, permeates his magical approach to film-making. His first film *Jubilee* (1978), 'Britain's only decent punk film', features a time-travelling John Dee.

1–2 February Imbolc, Imbolg, Candlemas, Saint Brigid's day. Marking the midpoint between the winter solstice and the spring equinox, Imbolc celebrates renewal and the burgeoning of new life: the invisible presence of spring's earliest signs. This is a time for cleansing, blessings, initiations and renewal of oaths. Out with the old and in with the new.

3 February Setsubun (Japan). Scatter soybeans at the shrine and at home to ward off bad luck and disease-bringing spirits. Wear demon masks and pelt family members with beans to shouts of 'In with the luck! Out with the demons!' A time of cleansing. Eat a number of beans equal to your age for good luck.

5 February 2023 Thaipusam, a festival celebrated by the Tamil community in the month of Thai, when the moon passes through the star Pusam and is at its brightest. After two days of ascetic preparations, today is the day of the 'burden dance', commemorating the day on which Parvati gave the warring god Murugan a javelin to vanquish the demon Soorapadman.

Saturday
4

Sunday
5

Soji
A Meditation on Zen Cleaning
by Shoukei Matsumoto

大掃除

In Japan, cleaning is called 'Soji' and valued as a way to cultivate our minds. In fact, Soji is beyond mere cleaning. Buddhist monks in a monastery put more time into practicing Soji than into practicing Zen meditation. Actually, Zen is not only about meditation but about your whole life.

A monk's day begins with cleaning. We sweep the temple grounds and gardens and polish the temple building. We don't do this because it's dirty or messy. We sweep dust to remove our worldly desires. We scrub dirt to free ourselves of attachments.

One important thing Soji practice tells us is that we never complete cleaning. Just as leaves begin to fall right after you sweep, desires begin to accumulate right after you refresh your mind. We continue cleaning the gloom in our hearts, knowing that we will never end it.

How can you change your daily housework into an opportunity to contemplate yourself? I recommend that you have your own ritual when you start cleaning. In my case, I give prayer and chant a short mantra to a little Buddha statue before cleaning. Once you make it your daily routine, it protects you from evils. This is the power of routine.

February

Week 6

Monday
6

Tuesday
7

Wednesday
8

Thursday
9

Friday
10

5–6 February 2023 Tu B'Shevat. Taking place on the 15th of the month of Shevat, this holiday is also known as the 'New Year for Trees'. Plant trees in memory of loved ones and eat grapes, figs, pomegranates, olives and dates. This holiday is focused on responsible stewardship of the Earth, with some contemporary versions of the Tu B'Shevat seder emphasising environmentalist concerns. 'Man is a tree of the field.'

Early February Look out for the young shoots of nettles, chickweed and cleavers; these early spring weeds are common in temperate zones, with a plethora of uses as anti-inflammatories, diuretics, for lymphatic support and as sources of minerals and vitamins. Prepare in teas, salads and pestos.

9 February 1944 Alice Walker, novelist, short story writer, poet and activist, is born in Putnam County, Georgia. Through her work on Vodou for *The Revenge of Hannah Kemhuff*, she discovers Zora Neale Hurston, bringing her writing to a new generation. 'We do carry an inner light, an inner compass and the reason we don't know we carry it is because we've been distracted.'

10 February Feast of Saint Paul's Shipwreck (Malta). In 60 CE, after his ship is caught in a storm on the way to Rome from Jerusalem, strong winds blow Saint Paul's vessel onto Malta's shores. While in Malta, Paul is bitten by a venomous snake while standing by a fire, yet remains uninjured while the locals stand in awe. Commemorative festivities involve processions, feasts and ceremonies.

12 February 1964 Gerald Gardner dies on a boat en route to Tunisia. Widely considered 'the father of Wicca', he brought witchcraft to public attention and founded the tradition of Gardnerian Wicca.

Notes

Saturday
11

Sunday
12

February

Week 7

Monday
13

☽ in Scorpio

Tuesday
14

Wednesday
15

Thursday
16

Sun conjoins Saturn

Friday
17

14 February Trndez (Armenia). A feast of purification in the Apostolic Church, held forty days after the birth of Jesus. A Christianised form of pre-existing pagan solar and fire worship symbolising the birth of the fire-god Vahakn. Build a bonfire and jump through to strengthen the heat of the sun, banish the cold.

15 February 1638 Birth of Zeb-un-Nissa, Sufi poet and Mughal princess. Writing under the pseudonym 'Makhfi', she was imprisoned for the last twenty years of her life by her father, the Mughal emperor Aurangzeb. Her many writings were collected posthumously and published as *Diwan-i-Makhfi*, the *Book of the Hidden One*.

16 February 1878 Pamela Colman Smith, artist, writer and occultist, is born in Pimlico, London. Also known as Pixie, Smith illustrated and brought to life the Rider-Waite tarot deck. Still the most popular 78-card deck in use today, other suggested names for this set to reflect her essential contribution include the Rider-Waite-Smith, Waite-Smith and Waite-Colman-Smith. 'Find eyes within, look for the door into the unknown country.'

18 February 1934 Audre Lorde, feminist, writer, poet and teacher, is born Audrey Geraldine Lorde in New York City. Lorde defied ways of knowing defined by 'racist, patriarchal, and anti-erotic society' by drawing on the I Ching, tarot and traditions of African goddesses and warriors.

18 February 2023 Maha Shivaratri (South Asia), the Great Night of Shiva. The most significant of the twelve annual Shivaratris honouring the Hindu god Shiva sees devotees fasting, meditating, keeping night vigils and making pilgrimages to temples of Shiva throughout the night.

Notes

Saturday
18

Sunday
19

February

Week 8

Monday
20

● in Pisces

Tuesday
21

Wednesday
22

Thursday
23

Friday
24

21 February 2023 Mardi Gras. Carnival celebration beginning after the Epiphany and culminating on the day before Ash Wednesday, which opens the fasting of Lent.

22 February 2023 Ash Wednesday, a day of prayer, fasting and repentance. Ash is placed on the forehead: 'Remember that you are dust, and to dust you shall return.' In Haiti, the start of Rara Carnival's street processions, dances and songs, vaccines, trumpets, bells, maracas, drums, *güiras*, *güiros*. Haitians call it 'Vodou on the road', a victory of the spirit against the spectres of slavery.

February Look just below the surface of still waters to spot ghostly, jelly-like clouds of frogspawn – an early sign of spring. Frogs have many attendant superstitions, often attached to the weather; their croaking is believed to herald storms. Some cultures believe that the death of a frog brings floods and heavy rains, while others say that it will bring drought. Likewise, a frog coming into your home may bring good fortune, bad luck, a spell or a curse.

21 February 921 Abe no Seimei, *onmyōji* for the court, astrologer and legendary figure in Japanese folklore, is born. Court practitioners of *onmyōdō* – an esoteric cosmology combining occultism and natural sciences – were responsible for divination and protection of the city from evil spirits and keeping track of the calendar.

24 February Dragobete (Romania). Celebrating love, romance and the beginning of spring, this Romanian Valentine's Day is rich in traditions and superstitions. It is believed to originate in ancient myths in which Dragobete is a demi-god, often seen riding a white horse during daylight hours. A symbol of spring and light, Dragobete's magical presence makes trees flower, creatures multiply, and people become lovers.

Saturday
25

Sunday
26

February
March

Week 9

Monday
27

☾ in Gemini

Tuesday
28

Wednesday
1

Thursday
2

Friday
3

27 February 1861 Rudolf Steiner, founder of Anthroposophy, of the biodynamic approach to agriculture, educator, philosopher, esotericist, architect, social reformer, playwright, is born in Kraljevec, present-day Croatia. A polymath who had a significant influence on many people and disciplines, Steiner is best known for his legacy of Steiner schools.

3 March Hamauri (Okinawa, Japan), a Ryukyuan day of purification at the beach for women and girls only. Walk on the beach and collect shells. A holiday for eating rice cakes and mugwort.

Early March Wai Khru festival (Thailand). Wat Bang Phra is a Buddhist monastery in the Nakhon Pathom province famous for SakYants tattoos, which bestow mystical powers, protection or good luck. On this day people queue to receive a tattoo or have their tattoo re-empowered. After completion, the tattoo is blessed and an incantation is blown over it.

March A good time to sow vervain (*verbena officinalis*), a plant of Venus with Martian characteristics. Called 'tears of Isis' in ancient Egypt, it was woven into protective charms against the evil eye in Italy. Used mainly for protection and love magic, it germinates in about 3-4 weeks and likes full sun, rich soil and some space to grow.

5 March 1938 Lynn Margulis, evolutionary theorist, biologist, science author and educator, is born Lynn Petra Alexander in Chicago, Illinois. She will go on to revolutionise the scientific view of early cell evolution, with her 'serial endosymbiotic theory of eukaryotic cell development' overturning the modern concept of how life arose on Earth. She will also co-develop the Gaia hypothesis, which proposes that the Earth functions as a single, self-regulating system.

Notes

Saturday
4

Sunday
5

March

Week 10

Monday
6

Tuesday
7

☽ in Virgo
Saturn enters Pisces

Wednesday
8

Thursday
9

Friday
10

6 March 2023 Maka Bucha (Thailand) commemorates the assembly of over a thousand enlightened monks to be ordained by the Buddha. A popular ritual on this day is the candle ceremony: walk clockwise three times around the temple holding flowers, incense, and a lighted candle. Each circuit represents one of the core concepts of Buddhism: Buddha, Dharma and Sangha.

8 March International Women's Day, a good time to remember that the creators of alchemy were women. Mary the Jewess, Cleopatra the Alchemist and Hypatia – three alchemists who, between the first and third century, laid the foundations of the Great Work to come.

8 March 1890 Scottish social anthropologist and folklorist James G. Frazer writes the preface to the first edition of *The Golden Bough*. The book, originally in two volumes, will mushroom into a twelve-volume epic on fertility rites, human sacrifice, dying solar gods and their mystic marriage to the earth goddess.

9 March St. Maron's day (Maronite Church). Maron was a fourth-century Syrian hermit monk who lived in the Taurus Mountains near Aleppo, Syria. After his death, his following grew into the modern Maronites. Known for his simplicity and his extraordinary desire to discover God's presence in all things, Maron lived his life in the open air next to a temple he had transformed into a church.

Mid-March The beginning of Bysios, the month for consulting the Oracle at Delphi. She spoke on behalf of the Gods for more than twelve centuries, counselling petitioners from across the Hellenic world on everything from when to declare war to how to fix their sex lives.

Notes

Saturday
11

Sunday
12

March

Week 11

Monday
13

Tuesday
14

Wednesday
15

☽ in Sagittarius

Thursday
16

Friday
17

14 March 1879 Dita e Verës, a pagan Albanian holiday celebrating the passage from winter to spring. The deity Zana, also known as Diana or Artemis, comes out of the temple outside Elbasan on this day, breaking the clutch of winter. In the morning, eat the *ballakume* cookies baked in every house, then visit bonfires and parades around town.

15 March 2017 The Whanganui Māori tribe of the North Island of New Zealand have fought for 140 years for the legal recognition of their river as an ancestor. On this day, the river is finally recognised as having legal personhood.

15 March The Ides of March, the 74th day in the Roman calendar. Sacred to Jupiter and also to Anna Perenna, an old Roman deity of the circle or 'ring' of the year. The date gained infamy following the assassination of Gaius Julius Caesar in 44 BCE, after the politician and military general was warned to beware the day, probably by the haruspex seer Spurinna.

18 March The first day of the month of the Alder Moon in the Celtic Tree Calendar. Also called Fearn, Alder flourishes on riverbanks and is associated with the boundary between our world and magical spaces.

March 1927 *An Experiment with Time* by the aeronautical engineer John Dunne is published. The influential book argues for the occurrence of precognitive dreams and explains techniques for recording and analysing them. For Dunne, dreams do not foresee future events, only future experiences of the dreamer.

Notes

Saturday
18

Sunday
19

March

Week 12

Monday
20

Sun enters Aries

Tuesday
21

● in Aries

Wednesday
22

Thursday
23

Pluto enters Aquarius
Ceres enters Virgo

Friday
24

20 March 2023 Vernal equinox, the first day of spring when day and night are in equilibrium. In the wheel of the year it is Ostara, the second of the lesser sabbats, a time for sowing and planting.

20 March 2023 Nowruz – literally 'new day' – the Persian New Year. Beginning on the spring equinox, it marks the first day of Farvardin, the first month of the Iranian solar calendar. Nowruz has Iranian and Zoroastrian origins, but has been celebrated by many communities of different faiths for over 3,000 years in Western and Central Asia, the Caucasus, the Black Sea Basin, the Balkans, and South Asia. Celebrate by spring cleaning, visiting loved ones and gathering around the traditional Haft-sin table.

22 March 2023 Ramadan begins, lasting from one sighting of the crescent moon to the next. The ninth month of the Islamic calendar, Ramadan is observed by Muslims worldwide as a time of prayer, spiritual reflection and community focus. A common practice is fasting (*sawm*) from dawn to dusk, as well as devoting more time to prayer and acts of charity, improving self-discipline, and eschewing worldly activities. For Sufis, a key aspect of dedication is the rhythmic music of *zhiker*.

22 March 2023 Sarvadhari, Hindi New Year. One associated tradition is the 'first seeing', in which *kani* (dazzling arrangements of money, jewels, clothing, flowers, fruits and sweets) are arranged around shrines on the eve of the new year. At dawn, the matriarch will take blindfolded family members to the shrine, where the blindfold is removed so that their first sight of the year is auspicious. Catching sight of a mirror, which reproduces the *kani's* abundance, brings extra luck.

Notes

Saturday
25

Sunday
26

March
April

Week 13

Monday
27

Tuesday
28

Wednesday
29

◐ to Cancer

Thursday
30

Friday
31

March Jimsonweed, thornapple or datura (*datura stramonium*) can be sown around this time. Don Juan warns: 'She is as powerful as the best of allies, but there is something I personally don't like about her. She distorts men. She gives them a taste of power too soon without fortifying their hearts and makes them domineering and unpredictable. She makes them weak in the middle of their great power.' A plant of Saturn, good for binding and to be treated with care. Sow in rich soil when the weather is warm and grow in full sun.

28 March 1515 Teresa of Ávila, now Saint Teresa, Carmelite nun and mystic, is born in Ávila, Spain. 'To reach something good it is very useful to have gone astray, and thus acquire experience.'

1 April Veneralia, an ancient Roman celebration of Venus Verticordia (Changer of Hearts) and Fortuna Virilis (Bold Fortune). People seek divine guidance on marriages, romance and sex.

2 April 1968 Our Lady of Zeitoun's first appearance. A female figure in white is sighted on the roof of a Coptic church, the first of many mass Marian apparitions in Zeitoun, Cairo. The phenomenon recurs frequently for two years and is witnessed, filmed and photographed by the press and the Egyptian President.

Notes

Saturday
1

Sunday
2

April

Week 14

Monday
3

Tuesday
4

Wednesday
5

Thursday   in Libra
6

Friday
7

5 April 2023 Qingming (China), tomb-sweeping day. Families visit the tombs of their ancestors, clean and sweep tombstones, pray to the ancestors and offer each other remembrances of beloved deceased. Green tea made from leaves picked before this date ('pre-qingming') have a lighter and subtler aroma.

6 April 1917 Leonora Carrington, artist, surrealist painter, writer and a founding member of the Women's Liberation Movement in Mexico, is born in Clayton-le-Woods, Lancashire, UK. 'I've always had access to other worlds. We all do, because we dream.'

6 April 1744 Emanuel Swedenborg, Swedish Lutheran theologian, scientist, philosopher, revelator and mystic, starts receiving visions that culminate in his spiritual awakening and the writing of *The Heavenly Doctrine*. 'People are unaware that spirits even exist, let alone that angels are present with them.'

8–10 April 1904 In Cairo, British poet and occultist Aleister Crowley receives the *Book of the Law*, the central holy text of Thelema, from the disincarnate entity Aiwass. 'Had! The manifestation of Nuit/ The unveiling of the company of heaven/ Every man and every woman is a star/ Every number is infinite; there is no difference.'

9 April 1626 Death of Francis Bacon, philosopher and scientist, in London after catching a chill stuffing a hen with snow to test the effects of cold on the preservation and decay of meat. Theosophical and post-theosophical groups believe that he only staged his death and attended his own funeral in disguise. He then travelled to Transylvania to stay with the Hungarian royal family and alchemically achieved Ascension, immortality and eternal youth.

Notes

Saturday
8

Sunday
9

April

Week 15

Monday
10

Tuesday
11
Sun conjoins Jupiter

Wednesday
12

Thursday
13
☽ in Capricorn

Friday
14

Notes

13 April 1662 The first of four confessions that Isobel Gowdie gave during the Early Modern witch-hunts in Scotland. Gowdie's confessions portray a combination of devil and fairy lore, describing her coven's activities, carnal dealings with demons, meetings with the fairy queen and rhymes and charms used by local witches.

13–15 April Songkran (Thailand). Derived from the Sanskrit work *sankranti*, meaning astrological passage, this festival marks Thailand's new year. Throw jugs and buckets of water filled with fragrant herbs, washing away all that is evil.

14 April 2023 Festival of Vaisakhi. For Sikhs the day commemorates the formation of Khalsa panth of warriors under Guru Gobind Singh in 1699. For many Hindus, the holiday is known as Vaisakha Sankranti and celebrates the solar new year. In India, it is also a spring harvest festival, an occasion to bathe in sacred rivers such as Ganges, Jhelum and Kaveri, to visit temples and enjoy festivities.

14 April 1947 Dale Pendell, poet, ethnobotanist, alchemist and sage of the poison path, is born. 'If you let the alembic cool, metaphor becomes superstition.'

15 April 1953 On this day William Burroughs, writer, artist and Beat, returns from the jungle in Peru, reporting to Allen Ginsberg that he had successfully learnt the art of preparation and consumption of Ayahuasca. 'Man is an artifact designed for space travel. He is not designed to remain in his present biologic state any more than a tadpole is designed to remain a tadpole.'

Saturday
15

Sunday
16

April

Week 16

Monday
17

Tuesday
18

Wednesday
19

Thursday
20

● in Aries
Total Solar Eclipse in Aries

Friday
21

Mercury stations retrograde

18 April 1300 The Divine Comedy begins on the night before Good Friday with Dante lost in a dark forest, assailed by beasts and unable to find his way. The poet Virgil comes to his rescue and takes him on a journey to the underworld.

18 April 1947 Kathy Acker, feminist, experimental writer, 'punk poet', playwright, essayist, plagiarist and performance artist, is born Karen Lehmann in Manhattan, New York City. 'Every book, remember, is dead until a reader activates it by reading. Every time that you read you are walking among the dead, and, if you are listening, you just might hear prophecies.'

April 1989 *Taboo: The Sixth Sense*, a fortune-telling game, is released by Nintendo. The player inputs data to receive a tarot reading using the 78-card deck and the Celtic Cross layout. Ensuing divinatory games include *House of Tarot* (1991) and *Tarot Mystery* (1995).

20 April 1814 Georgiana Houghton, artist and medium, is born in Las Palmas de Gran Canaria in the Canary Islands. After the death of her sister, she becomes interested in spiritualism and starts to channel creative spirits, including Titian and angelic beings, who would draw by guiding her hand. 'In the execution of my Drawings my hand had been entirely guided by the spirits, no idea being formed in my own mind as to what was going to be produced.'

23 April 1922 Marjorie Cameron, artist, actress, poet and Thelemic occultist, is born in Belle Plaine, Iowa. After the death of her husband and magical mentor, rocket pioneer and fellow Thelemite Jack Parsons in 1952, Cameron will withdraw to the desert. Returning to Los Angeles a few years later, she will appear in Kenneth Anger's film *Inauguration of the Pleasure Dome* in 1954.

Saturday
22

Sunday
23

April

Week 17

Monday
24

Jupiter conjoins Eris

Tuesday
25

Wednesday
26

Thursday
27

☾ in Leo

Friday
28

29 April 1917 Maya Deren, Ukrainian-American experimental filmmaker, choreographer, dancer, theorist and ethnographer, is born in Kiev, Ukraine. A classic in Haitian ethnography, her detailed book *Divine Horsemen* ends with her own possession by the goddess Erzulie. 'The bright darkness floods up through my body, reaches my head, engulfs me. I am sucked down and exploded upward at once. That is all.'

30 April 1896 Anandamayi Ma is born as Nirmala Sunadri in present day Bangladesh. At twenty-six years old, Nirmala will enact her own spiritual initiation on a full moon night at midnight in midsummer, and become a renowned Hindu spiritual leader, believed by her many followers to have powers of precognition and faith healing.

30 April 1966 Anton LaVey ritualistically shaves his head, proclaiming the founding of the Church of Satan and 1966 to be the first year of the new age of Satan.

30 April – 1 May Walpurgis Night. The eve of the Christian feast day of Saint Walpurga, an 8th-century abbess in Francia hailed by German Christian for battling 'pest, rabies and whooping cough, as well as against witchcraft'.

Notes

Saturday
29

Sunday
30

May

Week 18

Monday
1

Pluto stations retrograde

Tuesday
2

Wednesday
3

Thursday
4

Friday
5

☽ in Scorpio
Penumbral Lunar Eclipse

1 May Beltane, May Day. Third of the great sabbats, originally a pastoral festival when livestock is driven out to summer pastures. Bonfires, maypoles, bouquets and garlands; fertility, creativity and sensuality.

May Hawthorn (*crataegus monogyna*) is in full bloom. The flowers on these bushes are a hallmark of May, and their thorny branches feature in May Day traditions all over the UK. Leaves, flowers and fruits are useful in herbal remedies, particularly regarding the blood and the heart. Culpeper noted that hawthorn is ruled by Mars, and that 'the thorn gives a medicine for its own pricking.'

5 May 2004 The Supreme Court of India upholds the decision to allow universities to offer advanced degrees in Vedic astrology, thus retaining its place as one of the sciences.

6–7 May 2023 The Eta Aquarids are visible, particularly in the Southern Hemisphere. The meteors are produced by dust from comet Halley, which has been observed at 75-year intervals since ancient times, including in 1066, when its passage was believed to have heralded the Norman conquest of England. The Aquarids are visible annually – this year, the bright light of the waning gibbous moon may obscure all but the brightest.

7 May 1940 Angela Carter, novelist, short story writer and journalist, is born in East Sussex, England. Carter's surreal stories, steeped in esotericism and fantasy, explore myth and gender. 'The invisible is only another unexplored country, a brave new world.'

Notes

Saturday
6

Ceres stations direct

Sunday
7

May

Week 19

Monday
8

Tuesday
9

Wednesday
10

Thursday
11

Friday
12 ☾ in Aquarius

8–9 May Lag BaOmer. Jewish holy day taking place on the 18th of the month of Iyar. Celebrates the passing of the second century CE Rabbi Shimon bar Yochai, the first to publicly teach the mystical dimension of the Torah known as the Kabbalah, and author of the Zohar. Celebrate with bonfires, parades, and family outings, on which children traditionally play with bows and arrows.

8 or 13 May Feast of Julian of Norwich, mystic and anchorite. On the brink of death she receives a series of visions of Christ and the Virgin Mary, revealing God's love for humanity through the figure of Jesus, that miraculously cure her. She will write these 'shewings' in *Revelations of Divine Love*, the earliest surviving book in English written by a woman, and dedicate her life to solitary prayer. She is also patron saint of ladies with cats.

Early May Forage bramble or blackberry leaves (*rubus fruticosus*) before or during flowering and lay to dry. Ruled by Venus and Scorpio, the leaves are attributed to the element of water. Although they have cooling properties they are said to be a mild aphrodisiac. Apply bruised leaves to burns, hemorrhoids and eczema. Or use with a black candle and black salt for protection and returning evil.

9, 11, 13 May Lemuria, ancient Roman festival to exorcise ill-meaning ghosts from the home. Get up at midnight and scatter black beans around the house. Scream nine times: 'These I send! With these beans I redeem me and my kin,' while the rest of the household clashes together bronze pots asking the spirits to be gone.

Notes

Saturday
13

Sunday
14

May

Week 20

Monday
15 — Mercury stations direct

Tuesday
16 — Jupiter enters Taurus

Wednesday
17

Thursday
18 — Jupiter square Pluto

Friday
19 — ● in Taurus

15 May 1998 The Tarot Garden, the life-work of the artist Niki de Saint Phalle, opens to the public. In Capalbio, Tuscany, the garden contains monumental figures representing the artist's understanding of the mysteries of the tarot. During the two decades of work she lived in the sphinx-like High Priestess structure – her bedroom resided in one of the breasts, the kitchen in the other.

May 1954 The first Kālacakra initiation by the 14th Dalai Lama in Lhasa, Tibet. The key text *Kālacakra Tantra* weaves together yoga, astrology, eschatology and physiology into a system for meditation leading to perfect enlightenment. 'As it is outside, so it is within the body.'

18 May 1048 Omar Khayyam, Persian mathematician, astronomer and poet, is born on this day in Nishapur, a major centre of the Zoroastrian religion. The poetry ascribed to him became hugely popular in English translation as *The Rubaiyat of Omar Khayyam* during the fin de siècle. 'Heaven and hell are inside.'

18 May 2023 Semik, ancient Slavic fertility festival linked to a cult of the dead. On this day the *rusalki* spirits leave their watery abodes to swing from birch branches. No swimming, instead they use magic circles, garlic and wormwood for warding. Funeral rites are performed for those who have not received them.

20 May 2023 Gawai Dayak (Malaysia/Indonesia). Among the Dayak, longhouses are cleaned and decorated, and vegetables gathered from the gardens and the surrounding jungle to banish the spirits of greed. Offerings to the gods are placed in room corners, always in odd numbers: cigarettes, rice cakes, glutinous rice. Later on, the sword dance and the singing of poems continue the thanksgivings.

Notes

Saturday
20

Sunday
21

May

Week 21

Monday
22

Tuesday   Mars square Jupiter
23

Wednesday
24

Thursday
25

Friday
26

Notes

22 May 1914 Interplanetary Earth arrival of Sun Ra, The Magic City, Birmingham, Alabama.

24 May 1899 Henri Michaux, poet, artist and psychonaut, is born in Namur, Belgium. *Misérable Miracle*, the first of three books about his explorations of mescaline, describes his initial series of experiments with the 'infinity-machine' over a period of six months starting in January 1955. 'In mescaline one finds an independent consciousness with its own world of images. One learns what it is both to have and not have a will.'

25–27 May 2023 Shavuot, the 'Feast of Weeks'. This Jewish holiday occurs on the sixth day of the Hebrew month of Sivan, concluding the seven-week Counting of the Omer that begins on the second day of Passover. In Orthodox rabbinic traditions, the date marks the revelation of the Torah to Moses at Mount Sinai on this date in 1314 BCE.

26 May 2023 Birthday of the Buddha (East Asia). In many East Asian countries Buddha's Birth is celebrated on the 8th day of the 4th month in the Chinese lunar calendar; the day is an official holiday in Hong Kong, Macau and South Korea. Japan celebrates on 8 April of the Gregorian calendar each year.

27 May 1589 On his way to Prague, the alchemist and hermetic philosopher Heinrich Khunrath meets John Dee, on his way back to England from Bohemia. He will later also meet Edward Kelley at the Habsburg court. The Renaissance historian Frances Yates considered Khunrath to be the link between Dee's philosophy and Rosicrucianism.

Saturday
27

☾ in Virgo

Sunday
28

May
June

Week 22

Monday
29

Tuesday
30

Wednesday
31

Thursday
1

Friday
2

Jupiter conjoins the North Node

Early June A good time to forage dandelions (*taraxacum officinale*). A plant of Jupiter, although attributed to Venus by Nicholas Culpeper. Pick the young flowers only and remove the green base to avoid bitterness. Good for teas, wines, vinegars and jellies. The roots can be foraged in autumn; they have a chthonic character and in root work are used for necromancy.

Early June Xoy (Senegal), the time when the *saltigue* priests and priestesses of the Serer religion come together to divine the future in front of the community. Through the ceremony, the saltigue give sermons about many aspects of the future including the weather, politics and economics.

2 June Feast day of Saint Elmo (Erasmus of Formia). Elmo is said to have continued preaching following a thunderbolt striking the ground beside him, an act that prompted sailors, often in danger from sudden storms and lightning, to claim him as their patron saint. The eerie, blue, electrical discharges sometimes seen at the mastheads of ships were read as a sign of his protection, and came to be called 'Saint Elmo's Fire'.

2 June 1743 Count Alessandro Cagliostro, occultist and adventurer, is born Giuseppe Balsamo in Palermo, Sicily. In the European courts of the time he becomes mysterious and glamorous figure performing magical healings, alchemical workings and scrying.

Notes

Saturday
3

Sunday
4

in Sagittarius

June

Week 23

Monday
5

Tuesday
6

Wednesday
7

Thursday
8

Friday
9

Notes

June Elderflowers (*sambucus nigra*) are in bloom. Pick the flower heads in the morning on a sunny day, about ten or fifteen should suffice. Clean your tools and surfaces thoroughly, dissolve sugar in water, add the flowers, some lemon juice and wine yeast (or experiment with wild yeast). Leave to ferment for about a week, then strain through a muslin cloth and transfer to a new container with an airlock. You can drink it after a couple of weeks but it gets better with time, if you can wait. Calms anxieties and fears, stimulates joy and aids recovery for yourself or others. Used for protection, prosperity and to encourage good health.

10 June Nalukataq (the North Slope Borough, Alaska). On this day Iñupiat Eskimo whaling communities give thanks to the whales and celebrate the success of the hunting season. Festivities include the blanket dance, when the community throws a dancer in the air using a huge stretched trampoline of seal skins.

10 June First day of the month of the Oak Moon in the Celtic Tree Calendar. In Ogham it is *Duir*, which some believe to mean 'door', the root word of 'Druid'. Dreaming of resting under an oak tree means you will have health and a long life. Carry an acorn in your pocket to ward off illness and bring luck.

June 1960 Carlos Castaneda meets the Yaqui man of knowledge Don Juan Matus at a Greyhound bus station in Arizona. Castaneda will write a series of books detailing his training under Don Juan and his own experiences in shape-shifting, journeying and the use of psychoactive plants.

Saturday
10

☽ in Pisces

Sunday
11

Pluto enters Capricorn

June

Week 24

Monday
12

Tuesday
13

Wednesday
14

Thursday
15

Friday
16

13 June 1866 Aby Warburg, historian of art and ideas, is born in Hamburg, Germany. Founder of the Warburg Institute, where the beautiful library contains much occult, anthropological, and historical knowledge, he placed magic at the centre of the study of iconography and the moving image. *Mnemosyne Atlas*, his last, unfinished work, maps constellations of symbolic images through an associative method of images to trace 'the afterlife of antiquity'.

13 June 1865 W. B. Yeats, poet and one of the foremost occultists of his time, is born in Sandymount, Ireland. A leading member of the Hermetic Order of the Golden Dawn, he and Crowley, both young and charismatic students, could not stand each other. Their rivalry culminated in a magical battle during the splintering of the order.

16 June 1880 Alice Bailey, psychic, astrologer and theosophical writer, is born Alice LaTrobe-Bateman in Manchester, England. One of the first people to use the term 'New Age', she describes the majority of her works as being dictated by a Tibetan Master of Wisdom.

16 June 1924 Idries Shah, author and teacher in the Sufi tradition, is born in Simla, India. Through his many books and translations of classical Sufi literature, he brings Sufi ideas to the West. Friends with the poet Robert Graves and with Gerald Gardner, during his lifetime Shah held court for anyone interested in Sufism at the Cosmo restaurant in North London every Tuesday evening.

17 June 1951 Starhawk, neo-pagan, ecofeminist and activist, is born Miriam Simos in St. Paul, Minnesota. 'Because everything is interdependent, there are no simple, single causes and effects. Every action creates not just an equal and opposite reaction, but a web of reverberating consequences.'

Notes

Saturday
17

Saturn stations retrograde

Sunday
18

● in Gemini

June

Week 25

Monday
19

Jupiter sextile Saturn

Tuesday
20

Wednesday
21

Ceres enters Libra

Thursday
22

Friday
23

21 June 2023 Summer solstice, midsummer. The first day of summer, when the day is the longest and the night shortest. The triumph of the sun offers fulfillment, fruition and the sharing of its bounty.

22 June 1951 The Witchcraft Act, 1735 is repealed in the UK. The last person convicted under the Act was the spiritualist Jane Rebecca Yorke in 1944.

22 June 1947 Octavia Butler, feminist and visionary science fiction writer, is born in Pasadena, California. Her pioneering work transforms the landscape of speculative writing, often blending elements of science fiction and African American spiritualism. 'All that you touch You Change/ All that you Change Changes you/The only lasting truth Is Change/ God Is Change.'

23 June 1889 Anna Akhmatova, poet, translator and memoirist, is born as Anna Andreyevna Gorenka in Odessa, Ukraine. In August 1946, Akhmatova is denounced by the Central Committee of the CPSU and publicly castigated as 'half harlot, half nun' for the 'eroticism, mysticism and political indifference' of her poetry, deemed 'alien to the Soviet people'. 'I'm silent. Silently, I'm ready. To be transformed, earth, into you.'

24 June Inti Raymi, Inca solar adoration in honour of the god Inti. During the Inca empire people gathered in Cusco on the winter solstice (on this date in the southern hemisphere). Llamas were sacrificed and the main square ran with blood and beer. Coca leaves were read and burnt during festivities held from dawn to dusk. Still celebrated in Indigenous cultures throughout the Andes.

Notes

Saturday
24

Sunday
25

June
July

Week 26

Monday
26

☾ in Libra

Tuesday
27

Wednesday
28

Thursday
29

Friday
30

Neptune stations retrograde

Late June A good time to gather the leaves and bark of the ash (*fraxinus excelsior*), a solar tree sometimes attributed to Venus. Hesiod claimed the first man was born from the ash tree and Yggdrasil, the world tree of the Norse, was an ash. The bark has a plethora of medicinal properties and the wood is traditionally used to make besoms, wands and staves. Sleep with the leaves under your pillow for prophetic dreams or leave in a bowl of water overnight to stave off illness.

27–28 June 2023 Day of Arafah, on the second day of the Hajj pilgrimage to Mecca. At dawn, pilgrims make their way to a granite plain southeast of Mecca where Muhammad gave his last sermon. It is the most important day of Hajj; here they 'stand before God' in contemplative vigil from noon to sunset.

29 June 2012 The fall of Timbuktu to the militant Islamic group Ansar Dine. They destroy mosques, mausoleums and libraries, including the Sidi Yahya's mausoleum whose doors were not supposed to be opened until the end of days. Residents run great risks to evacuate many of the Timbuktu Manuscripts: tens of thousands of ancient texts on religion, medicine, astronomy, history, poetry, philosophy and magic.

30 June Nagoshi no Harae (Japan), the great purification. Under the instructions of the priest, bow, pass through a circular ring of woven reeds in the yard, circle back to the front from the left, pass through again and now go to the right, and pass through one last time reflecting on your year. Thus you are cleansed of all impurities and warded for the year to come.

Notes

Saturday
1

Sunday
2

July

Week 27

Monday
3

○ in Capricorn

Tuesday
4

Wednesday
5

Thursday
6

Friday
7

4 July 2023 Tirgan (Iran). This ancient summer festival is celebrated annually on Tir 13, the fourth month of the Solar Hijri calendar. Celebrate by splashing water, dancing, reciting poetry, and serving traditional foods such as spinach soup and *sholezard*. Tirgan is associated with the dog star Sirius, the coming of the rains in Iran and the fertility they bring. For Zoroastrians it is customary to visit the Fire Temple to give thanks to Ahura Mazda, and to participate in a jashan or thanksgiving ceremony.

7 July Kupala Night and Ivan Kupala Day (Ukraine, Poland, Belarus, Russia). A pagan fertility rite adopted by the Orthodox Christian tradition sees mischief, practical jokes and roaming the forest in search of magical herbs in the night-time. Divination by water follows floating candles and flowers on the river.

7 July 1947 A rancher reports finding a flying disc in Roswell, New Mexico. In 1995 footage of a related alien autopsy emerges in London.

9 July 1962 Death of Georges Bataille, writer, philosopher and mystic, who explores the importance of limit-experiences like death, eroticism and excess. 'I remain in intolerable non-knowledge, which has no other way out than ecstasy itself.'

July Shinugu (Okinawa). Near Kunigami village in the northern part of Okinawa, men climb up the mountains to ask the mountain and sea gods for prosperity and good harvest. Afterwards they assume the godforms of the mountain by covering themselves with leaves and adopting red flowers as crowns, to then descend and purify the village borders.

Notes

Saturday
8

Sunday
9

July

Week 28

Monday
10

☽ in Aries

Tuesday
11

Wednesday
12

Thursday
13

Friday
14

10 July 1856 Nikola Tesla, inventor, engineer and futurist, is born in Smiljan, Croatia. Tesla invents the modern alternating current electricity supply system, the first remote control, and a radio years before Marconi. A genius who treats engineering like poetry, magic and art. 'If you only knew the magnificence of the 3, 6 and 9, then you would have the key to the universe.'

13 July 1527 John Dee, occultist, mathematician, astrologer and advisor to Queen Elizabeth, is born in Tower Ward, London. Through a series of workings with the scryer Edward Kelley, he enters into contact with the angels and receives a language and system to converse with them through visionary magic. 'The message is that all things are connected. We have animal aspects, anthropological aspects, plant-animal aspects.'

16 July World Snake Day. Snakes and serpents appear in most belief systems and folklores, often seen as being close to the divine. They can represent fertility, desire, passion and the creative life force, and their likenesses have been used as guardians of temples and other sacred spaces. As snakes are known for regularly shedding their skin, they are also symbols of rebirth, transformation, immortality and healing. The ancient Greek and Egyptian ouroboros (snake eating its tail) is a symbol of eternity and continual renewal, while in Hinduism kundalini (the dormant potential force in the human body) is a coiled serpent.

Notes

Saturday
15

Sunday
16

July

Week 29

Monday
17
● in Cancer
The North Node enters Aries
The South Node enters Libra

Tuesday
18

Wednesday
19

Thursday
20
Mars opposite Saturn

Friday
21

Notes

18 July 2023 The start of the New Islamic Year 1445, and of the holy month of Muharram.

19 July 2014 Call of 13 Shamans festival begins in Tuva, Siberia. Practitioners from South Korea, Kazakhstan, Chile, Peru, Mexico, Mongolia, Greenland and shamans from Russia unite to call spirits of the nine worlds and perform rituals for several days.

22 July 1894 Maria Sabina, *curandera*, is born in the mountainous region of Sierra Mazateca in Mexico. She is the first to allow Westerners to participate in the *velada*, a healing vigil which makes use of psilocybin mushrooms. Many travel to her village as a result, including Bob Dylan and John Lennon. She is later ostracised from her community and felt the ceremony had been desecrated. 'From the moment the foreigners arrived, the 'holy children' lost their purity.'

July 1915 Walter Benjamin, writer, philosopher and mystic of profane illumination and hash hazes, meets Gershom Scholem in the library of the University of Berlin, starting a lifelong friendship and intellectual partnership.

July Yarrow (*achillea millefolium*) is in full bloom. Forage on a dry day after the morning dew has evaporated. A wound herb associated with Venus, with astringent, healing properties. Also used for divination, yarrow was rubbed on the eyelids for prophetic vision and in China its stalks were used to cast the I Ching before the modern three coin method. Also used for protection and love spells – and some say shapeshifting.

Saturday
22

Eris stations retrograde

Sunday
23

Venus stations retrograde
Pluto conjoins the South Bending
Chiron stations retrograde

July

Week 30

Monday
24

Tuesday
25

☾ in Scorpio

Wednesday
26

Thursday
27

Friday
28

25 July 1572 Death of Isaac Luria, commonly known as Ha'ARI ('the lion'). Rabbi and Jewish mystic in Galilee in Ottoman Syria, he is considered the father of modern Kabbalah.

25 July 1946 Demetra George, astrologer, mythologist and teacher, is born in Chicago, Illinois. Hugely influential on contemporary feminist astrologers such as Chani Nicholas, her work incorporates spiritual feminism, astrology, archetypal mythology and transpersonal healing therapies. Her books include *Asteroid Goddesses*, *Mysteries of the Dark Moon* and *Finding Our Way through the Dark*.

Late July A good time to forage mugwort (*artemisia vulgaris*). Gather the upper part of the plant just before it flowers and hang it upside down to dry. A moon plant sacred to Artemis, use for dreamwork and as a potent antiparasitic and digestive. In Chinese medicine mugwort is used in moxibustion.

29 July 1951 *The Sunday Pictorial* runs a story titled 'CALLING ALL COVENS' announcing the opening of the Folklore Centre of Superstition and Witchcraft in Castletown on the Isle of Man. Founded by Cecil Williamson together with 'resident witch' Gerald Gardner, the centre will later move to its current location in Boscastle, Cornwall, and reopen as the Museum of Witchcraft and Magic.

30 July 1926 Betye Saar, artist, is born in LA, California. Saar's work explores a cyclical notion of time, in which history, experience, feeling and knowledge are continually reinvented and re-explored. 'I can no longer separate the work by saying this deals with the occult and this deals with shamanism or this deals with so-and-so… it's all together.'

Notes

Saturday
29

Sunday
30

July
August

Week 31

Monday
31

Tuesday
1

☾ in Aquarius

Wednesday
2

Thursday
3

Friday
4

1 August Lammas, the first of the three Wiccan harvest festivals. The grain harvest is complete and bread is baked from the new flour (hence the Christianisation 'Loaf-mass'). A time to recognise all sacrifices made to bring forth this harvest, to appreciate all effort spent.

5 August 2019 Death of Toni Morrison, novelist, essayist, editor and teacher, aged 88 in New York. The only African American writer and one of the few women to have received the Nobel prize for literature, Morrison's novels centre on the Black American experience and incorporate a celebration of Vodou. In her novel *Beloved*, a former slave called Sethe is haunted by an apparition from her past; spectrality and communication with ancestors enable healing and rebirth. 'Birth, life, death – each took place on the hidden side of a leaf.'

6 August 1934 Diane di Prima, feminist, Beat, poet, playwright, fat acceptance activist and alchemist, is born in Brooklyn, New York City. 'Out of the heart of the ineffable/ draw the black flecks of matter/ & from these/ the cold, blue fire.'

August Lychnapsia, a Roman adaptation of Egyptian rituals for the birthday of the goddess Isis, explicitly linking the Mysteries of Isis with the Imperial Cult. Lamps are placed at temples and for the dead at their tombs. 'I came to the boundary of death and, having trodden on the threshold of Proserpina, I travelled through all the elements and returned. In the middle of the night I saw the sun flashing with bright light, I came face to face with the gods below and the gods above and paid reverence to them from close at hand.'

Notes

Saturday
5

Sunday
6

August

Week 32

Monday
7

Tuesday
8   ☽ in Taurus

Wednesday
9

Thursday
10

Friday
11

12–13 August 2023 The Perseids are active in the night sky. Produced by comet Swift-Tuttle, the Perseids produce a large number of bright meteors, up to 60 per hour at their peak. This year's waning crescent moon should leave the skies favourably dark for this dazzling display, especially after midnight.

10 August 1880 Leila Waddell, violinist and occultist, is born in Bathurst, Australia. Famous as Aleister Crowley's muse and Scarlet Woman, and immortalised in *The Book of Lies*, she is recognised as a powerful magical figure in her own right: an author, magician and one of the founders of the original company of the Thelemic Rites of Eleusis.

10 August 787 Abu Ma'shar, early Persian astrologer, is born in Balkh, Khurasan (present day Afghanistan). Renowned as the greatest astrologer of the Muslim world, his astrology manuals exert a profound influence on Islamic intellectual history and, through translation, on Western Europe and Byzantium.

13–15 August 2023 Obon (Japan). Buddhist festival of the dead. In the blazing heat and the roaring sound of cicadas, there are family reunions at ancestral family lands, cleaning of the family graves, and praying at the household altar. Also dancing, though the form varies regionally.

Notes

Saturday
12

Sunday
13

Sun conjoins Venus

August

Week 33

Monday
14

Tuesday
15

Wednesday
16 ● in Lieu

Thursday
17

Friday
18

August 1849 Discovery of the Royal Library of Ashurbanipal, the last great king of the Neo-Assyrian empire, in Nineveh. Among the thousand fragments and clay tablets is the Epic of Gilgamesh in Akkadian.

August 1960 Timothy Leary travels to Mexico and consumes psilocybin mushrooms for the first time. The rest of his life will be dedicated to exploring the potential of psychedelics for both therapy and journeying. He will become one of the key figures of 1960s counterculture working on concepts such as transhumanism, space exploration and consciousness modelling. Nixon dubbed him 'the most dangerous man in America'.

17 August 1828 Maria Deraismes, freemason and pioneering force for women's rights, is born in Paris. Refusing to accept male-only membership, Deraismes co-founded her own Masonic Lodge.

August 1909 The theosophist Charles Webster Leadbeater meets a young boy on a beach of the Adyar river. Jiddu Krishnamurti will be educated by the Society to be the vessel for the next World Teacher, an advanced spiritual entity periodically incarnating to aid the advancement of humanity. Krishnamurti will later reject the messianic mantle to develop his philosophy independently.

Notes

Saturday
19

Sunday
20

August

Week 34

Monday
21

Tuesday
22

Wednesday
23

Mercury stations retrograde

Thursday
24

☾ in Sagittarius

Friday
25

22 August 2023 Double Seven (China). Also known as the Qixi Festival, this ancient festival is celebrated on the seventh day of the seventh lunar month, when two lovers are allowed their annual reunion on the Magpie Bridge. In lore, a cowherd fell in love with and married a celestial weaving maid, who was then forced to return to heaven. Moved by their suffering, a flock of magpies formed a bridge across the Heavenly River (the Milky Way), placed by the Queen Mother of the West to separate them, so that they could meet.

22 August 1881 Agnes Pelton, painter, is born in Stuttgart, Germany, to American parents. At the start of her artistic career she joins the Transcendentalist Painter Group, studies Theosophy and in later life becomes a practitioner of Agni Yoga. Pelton's paintings are concerned with the spiritual reality beyond physical appearances.

24 August 1899 Jorge Luis Borges, Argentinian writer, poet and translator, is born in Buenos Aires, Argentina. 'This web of time – the strands of which approach one another, bifurcate, intersect or ignore each other through the centuries – embraces every possibility. We do not exist in most of them. In some you exist and not I, while in others I do, and you do not.'

25 August 1900 Death of Friedrich Nietzsche, one of the gnostic saints of Thelema.

25–27 August Yoshida Fire Festival (Japan) takes place at Kitaguchi Hongu Fuji Sengen Shrine at the foot of Mount Fuji. It is said that the pregnant Goddess Konohanasakuya-hime, accused of infidelity by her deity husband Niniginomikoto, set fire to the room she was staying in and delivered three babies in the flames. People give thanks for the divine protection of the goddess and to appease Mt. Fuji's anger.

Notes

Saturday
26

Sunday
27

August
September

Week 35

Monday
28

Tuesday
29
Uranus stations retrograde

Wednesday
30

Thursday
31
☽ in Pisces

Friday
1

30 August 1797 Mary Shelley, writer, dramatist and science fiction pioneer, is born in London. *Frankenstein: or, The Modern Prometheus* blurs the boundaries of science, alchemy and occultism. 'Life and death appeared to me ideal bounds, which I should first break through and pour a torrent of light into our dark world.'

30 August 1907 Leonor Fini, surrealist, painter, novelist, designer, and illustrator, is born in Buenos Aires, Argentina. Known for her depictions of unruly, powerful women. 'Paintings, like dreams, have a life of their own and I have always painted very much the way I dream.'

31 August 1979 A three-day conference in Arizona marks the beginning of the queer neo-pagan Radical Fairies movement.

September Eleusinian Mysteries, annual rites and initiations performed at Eleusis for the cult of Demeter and Persephone. Given that all initiates swore secrecy, not much is known about the actual rites. With Persephone the participants descended into Hades to reemerge transformed. Aristotle tells us that 'initiates do not need to understand anything; rather, they undergo an experience and a disposition – become, that is, deserving'.

Notes

Saturday
2

Sunday
3

September

Week 36

Monday
4

Venus stations direct
Jupiter stations retrograde

Tuesday
5

Wednesday
6

☽ in Gemini

Thursday
7

Friday
8

8 September 1985 Death of Ana Mendieta, known for her earth-body artwork, after falling from her New York apartment under suspicious circumstances. 'My art is grounded on the belief in one universal energy which runs through everything – from insect to man, from man to spectre, from spectre to plant, from plant to galaxy.'

10 September 1886 H.D. or Hilda Doolittle, poet and novelist, is born in Bethlehem, Pennsylvania. H.D. believes she has inherited the psychic 'gift' through her mother's Moravian ancestors and pursues an independent esoteric path. Her séances – some with the medium Arthur Bhaduri, and some around a table that once belonged to William Morris – and engagement with practical Kabbalah, tarot and astrology, inform her works including Helen in Egypt and Hermetic Definition.

10 September 1993 The X-Files pilot airs. The cult TV show will come to represent the conspiratorial zeitgeist of the time.

September A good time to harvest rosehips. High in vitamin C and iron, the fruit of the rose bush belongs to both Jupiter and Venus and can be used to attract wealth and love. Drink in tea or use in a ritual bath for work concerning companionship, peace and healing discord.

Notes

Saturday
9

Sunday
10

September

Week 37

Monday
11

Tuesday
12

Wednesday
13

Thursday
14

Friday
15

● in Virgo
Mercury stations direct
Ceres enters Scorpio

12 September 1940 Discovery of the cave of Lascaux in France containing 17,000-year-old cave art.

13 September 1985 Death of Dane Rudhyar, French-born American author, modernist composer and humanistic astrologer. A pioneer of modern transpersonal astrology, he brings astrology and Jungian psychology together to postulate that the stars do not cause the effects seen in human life, but form a symbolic language of images synchronistically aligned to human beings.

14 September 1486 Agrippa von Nettesheim, German scholar, theologian, polymath and occultist, is born in Cologne, Germany. His *Three Books of Occult Philosophy* are among the most important works in the Western esoteric tradition.

15 September 2023 Rosh Hoshana – literally 'head of the year' – the Jewish New Year. Customs include sounding the *shofar* (a cleaned-out ram's horn) as prescribed in the Torah, following the prescription of the Hebrew Bible to 'raise a noise' on Yom Teruah. Celebrate by enjoying festive meals, including symbolic foods such as apples dipped in honey to bring in a sweet new year.

17 September Feast of St. Hildegard von Bingen, twelfth-century Benedictine abbess, mystic, medieval shaman, theologian, composer and natural scientist. From a young age she receives visions from God informing her theological, artistic and scientific works. 'The Word is living, being, spirit, all verdant greening, all creativity. This Word manifests itself in every creature.'

Notes

Saturday
16

Sunday
17

September

Week 38

Monday
18

Tuesday
19

Wednesday
20

Thursday
21

Friday
22

☾ in Sagittarius

18 September 2023 Hartalika Teej (Nepal and North India). One of many women-only Teej festivals to welcome the monsoon and celebrate the goddess Parvati. Festivities for the deity include dancing, singing, storytelling, playing on swings hanging from trees, sharing food and wearing henna.

23 September 2023 Autumnal equinox. The sun rises directly east and sets directly west: the beginning of autumn. In the wheel of the year it is Mabon, the second of the harvest festivals, when the fruits of the earth are celebrated and shared to ensure the sustained blessing of the Goddess.

24 September 2023 Yom Kippur. Also known as the Day of Atonement, this is the holiest day of the year in Judaism. The themes of this day are atonement and repentance, traditionally observed with a day-long fast and intensive prayer. According to Jewish tradition, God inscribes each person's fate for the coming year on Rosh Hashanah, and waits until Yom Kippur to 'seal' the verdict.

Late September The days after prolonged rain are the best for picking mushrooms. Walking through meadows and pastures grazed by sheep, one can spot liberty caps (*psilocybe semilanceata*), just one of the many psychoactive varieties found in Europe and the US. Illegal in most countries, you may have to be satisfied with greeting them and walking on.

Late September Juniper (*juniperus communis*) has been one of our closest magical allies since the Neolithic period. Now is a good time for foraging the berries of this 'solar shrub' but make sure to only pick the ripe ones, of a rich purplish blue colour. A purifier both medically and magically, good for the relief of UTIs and menstrual cramps, as well as the cleansing of spaces and magical tools.

Notes

Saturday
23

Sunday
24

September
October

Week 39

Monday
25

Tuesday
26

Wednesday
27

Thursday
28

Friday
29

in Aries

Notes

26 September Feast of St. Cyprian the Mage and Justina. A third-century pagan magician from Antioch and the young woman who converted him by resisting his love spells. Many grimoires of the 17th, 18th and 19th century are attributed to Cyprian by their writers.

26 September 1918 Death of Caroline Tracy Dye, or 'Aunt Caroline', a highly respected seer whose name is recognised in Arkansas and the Mid-South in the early years of the 20th century. Born in slavery, she is gifted the 'far-eye' from childhood and spends much of her life giving readings to the people crowded daily in her house in Newport.

26 September 1991 The Theatre of All Possibilities opens Biosphere 2 in southern Arizona.

29 September 2023 Mid-Autumn Festival (East and South East Asia), also known as Moon Festival or Mooncake Festival. This important celebration is held on the fifteenth day of the eighth month of the lunar calendar and has a history dating back over 3,000 years, when the autumn full moon was worshipped to give thanks for the harvest. Carry lanterns to light the path to prosperity and good fortune. Eat mooncakes with cassia wine.

30 September 1207 Jalālad-Dīn Muhammad Rūmī, or Rumi, Sufi poet and mystic, is born in Balkh (in present day Afghanistan). 'Listen! Clam up your mouth and be silent like an oyster shell, for that tongue of yours is the enemy of the soul, my friend. When the lips are silent, the heart has a hundred tongues.'

Saturday
30

Sunday
1

October

Week 40

Monday
2

Tuesday
3

Wednesday
4

Thursday
5

Friday
6

☽ in Cancer

2 October 1917 Rosaleen Norton, witch and visionary artist, is born in Dunedin, New Zealand. She led her own coven in Kings Cross, Sydney and was dubbed the 'Witch of Kings Cross' by the tabloid press.

Early October Jašn-e-Mehr. This ancient Persian and Zoroastrian festival takes place in autumn and is dedicated to Mehr, also known as Mithra, the Persian god of light and love. Celebrate by laying a colourful table with rosewater, sweets, flowers, nuts, pomegranates and apples. Throw handfuls of wild marjoram, lotus and sugar plum seeds over one another's heads while embracing.

8 October 1825 Paschal Beverly Randolph, African American doctor, medium and occultist, is born in New York City. Founder of the Fraternitas Rosae Crucis, the oldest Rosicrucian organisation in the US, he is one of the modern pioneers of sexual magic and erotic alchemy.

8 October 2019 Death of Andre Barbault, French astrologer and writer. Beginning his astrological studies aged 14, Barbault focuses on the planets' effects on global events. He gains notoriety shortly after his death for accurately predicting the coronavirus outbreak, having noted in 2011 that 'it may well be that we are seriously threatened by a new pandemic in 2020-21'.

Notes

Saturday
7

Sunday
8

October

Week 41

Monday
9

Tuesday
10

Wednesday
11

Photo stations direct

Thursday
12

Friday
13

9 October 1906 Ithell Colquhoun, British artist, occultist and pioneer surrealist, is born in Shillong, India. Her interests span from alchemy to druidism, from ceremonial magic to earth magic, from sigils to tarot.

11 October Old Michaelmas Day (British Isles). An Irish proverb goes: 'On Michaelmas Day the Devil puts his foot on blackberries.' Falling from the sky after being vanquished by the Archangel Michael, Lucifer landed on a blackberry bush and cursed the thorny bush, stomping and spitting on it. Consequently, blackberries should not be picked after this date.

13 October 1998 Publication of Erik Davis' *Techgnosis*, exploring the relationship between modern technology and spirituality, occultism, mysticism and psychedelic experience.

13 October 1917 The Miracle of the Sun, an event prophesied by three young shepherds, manifests in front of a large crowd in Fatima, Portugal. The appearance of the Virgin Mary is followed by strange solar phenomena: a dull silvery sun dancing around the sky, plunging towards the earth and beaming multicoloured rays.

October 1994 Klaus Schmidt arrives at the site of Göbekli Tepe, the oldest religious site in the world. He will dedicate twenty years to excavating the temple in the quest to reveal its many hidden secrets.

Notes

Saturday
14

● in Libra
Annular Solar Eclipse in Libra

Sunday
15

October   Week 42

Monday
16

Tuesday
17

Wednesday
18

Thursday
19

Friday
20

18 October 1616 Nicholas Culpeper, herbalist, physician and astrologer, is born in London. He spends much of his life trying to make herbal medicine accessible to the layperson, combining remedial care, foraging, medical astrology and humoral philosophy. He translates herbal texts into vernacular and writes how-to guides for people who cannot afford medical treatment, despite the ban on the publication of medical texts.

21 October The sun penetrates the sanctuary of the Great Temple at Abu Simbel, Egypt, illuminating three of the four colossal statues within. The Pharaoh is revitalised by the solar energy and deified next to the celestial gods Amon-Ra and Ra-Horakhty, while the statue of the underworld demiurge Ptah remains in darkness.

21 October Apple Day (UK), an annual celebration of apples and orchards. Mark the occasion with apple games in the garden, village fairs, cookery demonstrations and the consumption of juice and cider.

22 October 1919 Doris Lessing, novelist, is born in British-Zimbabwean Rhodesia. Best known for *The Golden Notebook*, which explores mental breakdown as a means of healing and liberation, she also writes space fiction and is drawn to Sufism after becoming disillusioned with Marxist materialism. 'Whatever you're meant to do, do it now. The conditions are always impossible.'

Late October Naga fireballs, also known as Mekong lights, are visible on the Mekong River in Thailand and Laos. Around Wan Ok Phansa (the last day of Vassa, the Buddhist Lent) mysterious glowing fireballs rise from the water into the air. The phenomenon is named after the *naga*, the mythical serpent beings who live in the river.

Notes

Saturday
21

Sunday
22

☾ in Capricorn

October

Week 43

Monday
23

Tuesday
24

Wednesday
25

Thursday
26

Friday
27

23 October 2023 Double Nine Day (China). As the ninth day of the ninth lunar month, this day has too much yang and is thus potentially dangerous. For protection, consume chrysanthemum wine or tea, wear dogwood (*cornus officinalis*) or hike up a mountain. In Korea it is instead Jungu, and the double nine signals a favourable day for viewing the changing colour of maples during autumn.

24 October 1931 Sofia Gubaidulina, Tatar-Russian composer, is born in Chistopol, Russia. She believes in the mystical power of music and treats musical space as a means of attaining unity with the divine through the careful architecture of the musical form.

26 October 1862 Hilma af Klint, Swedish artist, mystic and pioneer of abstract art, is born at Karlberg Palace, Solna, Sweden. Part of a group of women called 'The Five' who channel entities called the High Masters through séances. Her resplendent, intense paintings are visual manifestations of her spiritual explorations.

27 October 1932 Sylvia Plath, American poet, novelist and short-story writer, is born in Boston, Massachusetts. Her poem 'Ouija' describes the spirit Pan, often contacted by Plath and Ted Hughes, saying 'fame cannot be avoided', and that it will come at a price: 'You will have paid for it with your happiness, / Your husband and your life.'

26 October 2023 Stow Horse Fair (UK). This traditional gathering of nomadic and traveller communities takes place on the nearest Thursday to 12 May and 24 October, in Stow-on-the-Wold, Gloucester, UK. This fair dates back hundreds of years, the Charter having been granted in 1476.

Notes

Saturday
28

○ in Taurus
Partial Lunar Eclipse

Sunday
29

October
November

Week 44

Monday
30

Tuesday
31

Wednesday
1

Thursday
2

Friday
3

31 October The veil between the dead and the living is at its thinnest, allowing some communication. It is Halloween (All Hallows' Eve) marking the beginning of Allhallowtide, and in Mexico, the beginning of the Day of the Dead festival (Día de Muertos). Also Samhain, the first of the greater sabbats of Wicca and the last of the harvest festivals, when the Horned God completes the journey to the underworld. In all traditions, it is a time to venerate the ancestors.

31 October 1968 Women's International Terrorist Conspiracy from Hell (W.I.T.C.H.) hexes Wall Street, New York. The stock market reportedly falls by thirteen points the following day. 'If you are a woman and dare to look within yourself, you are a Witch.'

1 November Feast of Santa Muerte, Our Lady of Holy Death (Mexico). A saint of Mexican folk Catholicism, a robed skeleton whose patronage includes healing, financial security, protection from violence and safe passage after death. Particularly venerated by night-workers, criminals and LGBTQ people. Offer cigarettes, alcohol, flowers, candles and candy.

5 November At nightfall in the village of Shebbear, Devon, people carrying crowbars and lanterns approach the huge stone close to the village church. At the bells' toll they work on turning it over. The devil is said to live underneath the stone and 'turning the Devil's boulder' averts bad fortune for the following year. The stone is not of any type found locally and its origins are unknown.

Notes

Saturday
4

Saturn stations direct

Sunday
5

☾ in Leo

November

Week 45

Monday
6

Tuesday
7

Wednesday
8

Thursday
9

Friday
10

Notes

November 1913 Psychoanalyst Carl Jung begins his 'confrontation with the unconscious', beginning a decade of journeying into visionary states of consciousness. From his journals of his explorations, Jung created *The Red Book* or *Liber Novus*, which draws on his 1913–16 records, and was published posthumously in 2009. *The Black Books*, seven volumes of Jung's 1913–32 notebooks, were published in 2020.

November Sangdal Gosa (Korea), a ritual held in the tenth lunar month in honour of all gods overseeing the safety and peace of a household. It may be an informal rite officiated by the mistress of the house, or a more formal one for which a professional shaman is called. A golden rope is coiled around the house, a layer of red clay spread on the floor to protect the house from evil spirits, and rice cakes offered to the gods on an altar.

November A good time to harvest Horseradish, a digestive and circulatory stimulant and powerful anti-inflammatory, ruled by Mars. The root mustard oils create heat for easing aches and pains.

8 November Death of John Milton, poet. Satan is the indisputable protagonist of his epic poem *Paradise Lost*, starting with the war in heaven and ending with the more domestic drama of the fall of humanity. The Archangel Michael tells Adam and Eve that they may still find 'a paradise within thee, happier far' after Satan's revenge and their expulsion from Eden.

12 November 2023 Kali Puja (West Bengal, Orissa, Assam), festival for the goddess Kali celebrated on the new moon of the Hindu month of Kartik.

Saturday
11

Sunday
12

November

Week 46

Monday
13

● in Scorpio

Tuesday
14

Wednesday
15

Thursday
16

Friday
17

Notes

15 November 1886 René Guénon, intellectual and important representative of the traditionalist and perennialist schools, is born in Blois, France. He writes on metaphysics, the 'sacred science' and symbolism. 'The "end of a world" never is and never can be anything but the end of an illusion.'

16 November 1956 Terence McKenna, ethnobotanist, mystic, and psychonaut, is born in Paonia, Colorado. 'The Timothy Leary of the 90s', he wrote and talked about the use of psychoactive plants, shamanism, alchemy, language, extraterrestrials, technopaganism and metaphysics. 'What we call imagination is actually the universal library of what's real.'

16 November Hekate's night. The night on which Hekate leads the wild hunt and the night when we must leave offerings at the crossroads. After placing the offerings, never look back and do not go back to retrieve the plate. Very similar to the Greek deipnon held for her at every dark moon.

17 November 1875 The Theosophical Society is established in New York. Based largely on Helena Blavatsky's writings, the society is an esoteric religious movement aimed at spreading the timeless wisdom of ascended masters.

19 November 2023 Chhath Puja, an ancient Vedic festival still celebrated in Bihar and parts of Nepal, begins. The festival is dedicated to the worship of the sun god and his wife Usha and is celebrated by following a rigorous routine that lasts four days.

Saturday
18

Sun conjuncts Mars

Sunday
19

November

Week 47

Monday
20

☾ in Aquarius

Tuesday
21

Wednesday
22

Thursday
23

Friday
24

22 November 1963 On this day Aldous Huxley is on the brink of death and unable to speak. His wife obliges his written request, 'LSD, 100 µg, intramuscular', and he dies a few hours later.

23 November 1221 Alfonso X of Castile, a King of Castile, León and Galicia, is born in Toledo, Spain. He fosters the translation of many Arabic and Latin manuscripts pertaining to astrology and magic including the *Picatrix*, a grimoire of talismanic and astrological magic which will influence in the Western esoteric tradition.

23 November 2023 Held on the same day as Thanksgiving in the US, the National Day of Mourning remembers the 1637 Pequot Massacre and all those Native Americans who lost their lives and culture through colonisation.

26 November 1865 Publication of Lewis Carroll's *Alice in Wonderland*, a plunge down the rabbit hole and out of the reality tunnel. 'Imagination is the only weapon in the war against reality.'

26 November 2023 The Lobpuri Monkey Festival usually occurs on the last Sunday of November. Lobpuri, an ancient city in Thailand with many ruins from the Khmer Empire, is host to a banquet for over three thousand long tailed macaques, honoured as descendants of the god Hanuman.

Notes

Saturday
25

Mars square Saturn
Ceres enters Sagittarius

Sunday
26

November
December

Week 48

Monday
27

☉ in Gemini
Eris conjoins the North Node

Tuesday
28

Wednesday
29

Thursday
30

Friday
1

November 1948 The French anthropologist Marcel Griaule publishes *Dieu d'Eau*, in English *Conversations with Ogotemmeli*, comprised of his conversations with a blind Sudanese Dogon sage over thirty-three days. Griaule notes that Dogon star lore is incredibly advanced and includes phenomena not visible to the naked eye. In 1976 Robert Temple publishes *The Sirius Mystery*, using the Dogon case in support of the ancient astronaut theory

28 November 1757 William Blake, poet, painter and visionary mystic, is born in Soho, London. 'If the doors of perception were cleansed every thing would appear to man as it is, Infinite. For man has closed himself up, till he sees all things thro' narrow chinks of his cavern.'

30 November 1943 Jerry Hunt, composer and occultist, is born in Waco, Texas. One of the pioneers of electronic music, he composed using homemade electronic apparatuses, ritual and magical principles from the Goetia, alchemy, Vodou, tarot and Qabalah. He was particularly fond of John Dee, even using the Enochian tablets as compositional method.

1 December 1973 First posthumous exhibition of the Swiss healer and visionary artist Emma Kunz in Aarau, Switzerland. She described her creative work as 'shape and form expressed as measurement, rhythm, symbol and transformation of figure and principle'. AION-A, the healing stone discovered by Kunz, is still used widely.

Notes

Saturday
2

Sunday
3

December

Week 49

Monday
4

Tuesday
5   ☽ in Virgo

Wednesday
6   Neptune stations direct

Thursday
7

Friday
8

4 December Feast of Changó or Santa Barbara (Cuba). One of the most important Orishas of Santería, Changó is owner of fire and thunder, quick to anger and full of virility, passion and power. Call him by shaking a maraca and praying at his altar; he likes bananas, okra, red palm oil and *amalá* (cornmeal dumplings).

Early December A good time to start mandrake (*mandragora officinarum*) seeds for your poison garden. Ally of witches, mandrake is ruled by Saturn and sacred to Hekate, although it also has a relationship to Mercury. Sow at solstice and persevere; true to its Saturnian character mandrake is hard to germinate and might take months or even years to sprout.

6 December 1890 Dion Fortune, occultist, magician, Qabalist and novelist, is born Violet Mary Firth in Llandudno, Wales. 'The driving forces of the universe, the framework upon which it is built up in all its parts, belong to another phase of manifestation than our physical plane, having other dimensions than the three to which we are habituated, and perceived by other modes of consciousness than those to which we are accustomed.'

10 December 1968 Thomas Merton, American Trappist monk, theologian, mystic, poet and activist, dies in Thailand. A prolific writer, Merton produces more than 50 books over 27 years and countless essays. He is a proponent of interfaith understanding, exploring Eastern religions through his study of mystic practice, and writing books on Christianity's relationship with Zen Buddhism, Confucianism and Taoism – an unusual topic at the time, particularly within the religious orders. 'Every moment and every event of every man's life on earth plants something in his soul.'

Notes

Saturday
9

Sunday
10

December

Week 50

Monday
11

Tuesday
12   ● in Sagittarius

Wednesday
13   Mercury stations retrograde

Thursday
14

Friday
15

12 December The mischievous Yule Lads begin to harass the Icelanders, for the thirteen days before Christmas Day. Their mother is Grýla, a child-eating giantess who lives in the mountains with the huge, ferocious Yule Cat.

14 December 1887 Xul Solar, Argentine artist, writer, astrologer and inventor of languages, is born in San Fernando de la Buena Vista, Argentina.

14 December 1503 Nostradamus, astrologer, seer and physician, is born in Saint-Rémy-de-Provence, France. The most famous oracle of all time; his *Les Propheties*, a collection of 942 poetic and prophetic quatrains, has rarely been out of print in the past five centuries.

16 December 1908 Remedios Varo, artist, feminist, surrealist, mystic, alchemist and naturalist, is born in Anglès, Spain. Her work fuses her interest in the work of Jung, Gurdjieff, Ouspensky, Theosophy and Sufism together with her own mystic explorations.

17 December Saturnalia, a Roman festival for the god Saturn. For the poet Catullus it was 'the best of days'. Sacrifices are made at the temple, a public banquet held, gifts exchanged, hierarchy and the law upturned. Gambling is permitted, partying ubiquitous, slaves are served by their masters, free speech flowing with the wine – all under the capricious orders of the King of the Saturnalia.

Saturday
16

Sunday
17

December

Week 51

Monday
18

Tuesday
19

☽ in Pisces

Wednesday
20

Thursday
21

Friday
22

Mid December A good time to harvest mistletoe (*viscum album*), a Sun herb that fights against despair and is used for protection against disease, lightning and fires. Rudolf Steiner called the herb 'aristocratic' and 'bohemian', due to its surviving paristically and living by its own rhythms.

21 December Winter solstice, the longest night. From here on the days get longer and the nights shorter. A time for new beginnings. Wiccans and Pagans celebrate Yule, the first of the sabbats, the rebirth of the Horned God. Rituals and dancing at Stonehenge until dawn. In 2012, the arrival of the singularity, according to Timewave Zero.

Approx. 21 December Pegrytti (Chukotka), a festival celebrated by Chukchi herders and hunters in northeastern Siberia. Festivities start when the star Pegrytti (Altair) appears in the Polar night – the harbinger of the return of warmth and sunlight. Fire is made by a fire plank passed down the male lineage, and the night sees dancing and reindeer sacrifice.

25 December 1642 Isaac Newton, physicist, mathematician, astronomer and alchemist, is born in Woolsthorpe-by-Colsterworth, Lincolnshire, England. It is only now that Newton's alchemical work is being recognised; of the manuscripts left behind, approximately half are religious, while one tenth are alchemical and eschatological predictions.

24 December The first day of the Celtic Tree Calendar, the beginning of the month of the Birch Moon. Time to look towards the light once more.

Notes

Saturday
23

Sunday
24

December

Week 52

Monday
25

Tuesday
26

Wednesday   ☉ in Cancer
27   Chiron stations direct

Thursday
28

Friday
29

25 December The birth of the sun; in ancient Rome, Dies Natalis Solis Invicti, meaning the 'birthday of the unconquered sun'. The time between the winter solstice and today also sees the Babylonian celebrations for Dumuzid/Tammuz, another solar god with dying and resurrecting patterns. Also the birth of Jesus, whose story follows in similar footsteps.

27 December 1882 Mina Loy, feminist, artist, writer, poet, playwright, is born in London. Her work aimed to transcend conventional ways of perceiving reality through mysticism and intuition. 'Our person is a covered entrance to infinity.'

27 December 1571 Johannes Kepler, mathematician, astronomer and astrologer, is born in Weil der Stadt, Germany. His legacy, including his discovery of three laws – 'celestial harmonies' – of planetary motion, transforms scientific thought and laid the groundwork for modern spaceflight, and he's a firm believer in the direct influence of the planets over human vicissitudes. In 1595 he successfully forecasts a peasant uprising, a Turkish invasion and a bitter frost. About 800 horoscopes written by him survive.

29 December 1926 Death of Rainer Maria Rilke, poet, in Montreux, Switzerland. 'The work of the eyes is done. Go now and do the heart-work on the images imprisoned within you.

December 1945 Discovery of the Nag Hammadi Library. Two brothers find an earthenware vessel containing several papyri while digging for fertiliser near the Jabal al-Ṭārif caves in Egypt. The papyri surfaced slowly on the market, one bought as a present for Carl Jung and now known as the Jung Codex. The library includes a large number of 'Gnostic Gospels', such as the Gospel of Thomas, which are fundamental to contemporary understanding of Gnosticism.

Notes

Saturday
30

Sunday
31

Jupiter stations direct

Appendix

Mercury Retrograde Acclimation Spread
by CAConrad

1
EARS
Aimed at tongues

2
INTUITION
Giant invisible ears

5
TALKING BACK
We need this better

6
THE WORK
Pulsing in the pentacle

3
VOICE
Ferment not foment

4
OLD FRIEND
Feel this message

Mercury retrograde occurs when Mercury appears to move in reverse, as its 88 day cycle around the Sun overtakes Earth's slower, 365-day orbit. During this astrological phase, wrong addresses, wrong dates, missed appointments, arguments and emotional chaos are at the heart of an unaware soul. Hearing and being heard can be more difficult during these times, as the god of communication is away from His post.

There is nothing to fear; think of this as an opportunity to master our attention. Instead of worrying about Mercury's trajectory, let's embrace Him! Prepare for the reading by making tea with some of the god's favourite flavours: star anise, cinnamon and lemon. Let's chew a little of His favourite herb, dill, before touching the cards. Draw wings on our ankles, whatever brings extra joy before casting the lot.

The card spread moves widdershins (that is, counter-clockwise, or against the path of the Sun) to honour Mercury's heavenly U-turn. It is an excellent time to consider the symbol of His caduceus, often confused for the healing staff of Asclepius. Mercury protected thieves, which is very curious – wealthy healthcare corporations incorrectly replace the healing staff with His caduceus. May our tarot cards clear the lens for the season of Mercury's reversal.

1. EARS - aimed at tongues

Mercury retrograde is about listening, but capitalism's orgy of consumption is a highly evolved distraction; no wonder so many people fear this cosmic cycle that demands our mindfulness. Our first card reveals the current state of our ears and what changes we might need to make for a smoother experience.

2. INTUITION - giant invisible ears

'I wish I had listened to my intuition' is not something we want to hear ourselves say. Always remember the triangular rule of intuition: listen, trust, act. Acting can require courage, and this card can show us how to embrace it with confidence. Consider this an evaluation of our follow through tools and abilities.

3. VOICE - ferment not foment

This card can tell us if we have been speaking too much, listening too little, or if we have a clear path ahead. We must remember not to sign important documents during the retrograde cycle: Mercury is the god of connecting us to our desired goals, and He is going backward at the moment, so hold tight. However, it is a terrific time to renegotiate contracts, do editing work, and process issues with other people, provided we work hard to emphasise ears over voice. Let this card show us the present condition of our communication skills.

4. OLD FRIEND - feel this message

Mercury retrograde is the perfect time to rendezvous with old friends. Since the god of connection is on vacation, we can turn to old relationships and revitalise bonds with loved ones. Before pulling this card, let's close our eyes and see their face. Hear their laugh, the way they walk, the foods we have shared, every and any detail. The card can give us a glimpse of the possibility of growth from slipping back into the path with them. Keep a steady memory focused on their smile throughout the day, see if they receive our psychic message and contact us.

5. TALKING BACK - we need this better

Let this card show us the crucial help we may need to move onward by addressing old wounds. Here is a conversation that can educate us on how to better carry the burden, or drop it on the ground and walk away forever.

6. THE WORK - pulsing in the pentacle

This card sits safely inside the belly of the pentacle formed by the first five. Let it show us how to proceed with creative projects and remarry our imaginations as often as possible to forge irrepressible strength. I am a poet, and when I have a poem with stubborn problems, I know that if I conjure the required patience and attention, it will be magically solved when we enter a Mercury retrograde cycle.

Tarot Spread: Refusing the Call
by T. Susan Chang

WHAT IS ON OFFER?	**WHY AM I REFUSING IT?**	**WHAT IF I SAID YES?**

'The image depicts reluctance, obliviousness, even boredom; the immobile figure at its center seems to be past caring. In his description of the hero's journey, this is the moment Joseph Campbell describes as the refusal of the call.' –
36 Secrets: A Decanic Journey through the Minor Arcana of the Tarot

This spread is for those pivotal moments when we may feel called to make changes in our lives, but we find ourselves hesitating. For many of us, the crises of the past few years have dampened our readiness to act, and the very prospect of change can feel fraught. This simple spread can help cast a spotlight on our reluctance, and perhaps overcome it.

1   **Find the Ace of Cups and Four of Cups.** Set them aside where you can see them. The three remaining cards will be random draws.

2   **What is on offer?** The Ace is an opportunity: a call to adventure or surrender. You must choose whether or not to accept it. If you don't, it may not come again

3   **Why am I refusing it?** Is it fear? Common sense? Not feeling worthy? Embarrassment? You might be right to say no. Or you might be wrong.

4   **What if I said yes?** You certainly don't have to, but it's worth asking the question. If you knew what was to come, you might change your mind.

Tomato Chutney: Ritual for Remembering
by Himali Singh Soin

This tomato chutney recipe-ritual is good for taking you back to a person or a place that is fraught but that you need. And needs you. It clarifies doubt, it makes you feel held.

I like to make this chutney on warm summer days when I need that particular, indirect, Delhi strength. I combine it with a goat cheese salad and a charcoal sourdough, or rye toast. It's light on the stomach and revitalising in a pacifying way.

I ring my mother or grandmother every time I cook it: the phone call feels like a rite of passage, a land acknowledgement.

I come from a city with a grand, masculine centre with big, wide roads and bright barriers that keep out anything soft or subtle. Delhi's mughal homes had *zenanas*, rooms specifically for women, tucked away in the back corners behind trellised screens. Princesses and their attendants, courtesans, trans women, all spent time there together. The impossibilities between the classes were momentarily suspended. It was in these *zenanas* that hushed, peaceful forms of resistance grew.

As a child, I played in the peripheries: climbing Gulmohar trees to pick their flower buds and battle with the stamens inside, a game no one knew the name of or the rules to; counting parakeets on the lacerated lapis domes of tombs till the big, dusty, orange sun faded into white and then made as many wishes. Mostly, I made a mess in the modern *zenana*, my grandmother's kitchen. Charmed by the bright colours of the *masala daan*, I produced mysterious pastes out of turmeric and chilli and pink salt, considering myself some kind of alchemist. I insisted that if we all adorned our eyebrows and lips and earlobes and wrists with them, they'd ward off evil.

I left for college and the city began to choke on its own modernity. By the time I returned, it had met its sooty fate. Everything wheezed behind a film of smog and hot, bent light.

Those early activities feel like life lessons now, shielding me from the violences of a neocolonial state. A kind of warmth of spirit mixed with a fiery aggression. You learned to do the work, you also trusted that the work will get done.

The women in my family had a recipe for it. An anti-imperial, liberationist tomato chutney.

टमाटर चटनी
Timator chutney *(to cleanse the air and listen to the earth)*
This recipe serves 6

2 tbsp olive oil
1½ tsp *panchphoran* (an equal part mixture of cumin, fenugreek, nigella, black mustard and fennel seeds)
1 inch cube of ginger, peeled and finely chopped
6 good-sized cloves of garlic, ground in a mortar and pestle
6–8 bright, juicy, heirloom tomatoes, diced at the seam or quartered
2 whole, hot, dried red chillies
1 tsp Himalayan salt
1 tablespoon jaggery or honey
2 strawberries cut into ½ in cubes
1 whole fresh green chilli
Garnish of fresh cilantro leaves

Begin by picturing the tomatoes on their vines. Heat the oil in a pot over a medium flame. Stir in garlic and ginger til brown. Scatter the panchphoran mixture in the pot. They will begin to sizzle and pop in seconds: make sure they don't burn. Now put in the red chillies. Then toss in the tomatoes and the salt. Cover and simmer on a low flame. Stir occasionally.

About 20 minutes later, once the tomatoes look like they're becoming softer, mix in the jaggery, strawberries and green chilli. Mash them gently. Leave the lid open and cook on a low-medium flame till the chutney looks strong and bright.

Garnish with fresh coriander. Serve hot or cold, with any cuisine.

The slight sourness of the chunks of strawberry have been adapted from the original recipe which contains apricot chunks and can be replaced with plums in the autumn. We shift things a little: enough to keep our concoctions illegible to the oppressor and in a room of our own. The chilli and jaggery, the dash of salt, topped with coriander magically summons life in the narrow, windy streets, where everything bumps into you and you are caressed by everything you pass. It asks you to allow chaos in. The steam from tea in the terracotta *kullad* encounters the tailor's perpetual pedal, the silent cardamom and the false stitch perfectly porous. It says: go out into the green. Know the world with your senses only. It allows us a new openness. Think of it as a non-binary, border-defying, hyper-sensorial, pleasure inducer.

Ritual for a Bright Beginning
by Pam Grossman

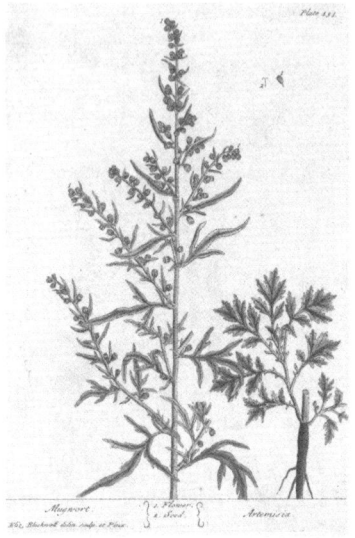

Image: Mugwort illustration, Elizabeth Blackwell, 1739

New Year rituals are inspiring to me because they posit that, no matter our collected experiences or current circumstances, with a bit of mystical intention we can start anew. I love the promise of a planted seed, a clean slate, a sloughing off of the skin to expose a deeper, gleaming layer.

As I've gotten older, I've realised that the magic of the New Year is something I celebrate many times over 365 ¼ days, depending upon which calendar I'm following. There's 1 January of the Gregorian calendar, my own solar return in February, Rosh Hashana of my ancestors' Jewish lunar calendar, and Samhain – Witches' New Year – on the seasonal Pagan Wheel. Each of us may choose to follow our own individual, holographic calendar – a palimpsest of holy moments marked throughout a multiplicity of histories and sacred cycles.

Certainly, we can sanctify any moment of our lives and deem it a fresh start. When witches cast a magic circle, we traditionally begin by calling in the spirits of air in the East, direction of the rising sun, direction of thought, of voice, of breath. With each looped pairing of inhale and exhale, we bring our attention to the possibility of transformation. Circles casting circles.

Still, if you are looking to align your new beginning ritual with a celestial occasion, you can do no better than working with a new moon. Each month, this heavenly phase invites us to open ourselves up to ignited action, first steps and a readiness for positive change.

For this Bright Beginning Spell, you will need:

- Mugwort – also known as *Artemisia vulgaris*, this herb induces visions, lunar magic and vivid dreams, and is associated with the Greek moon goddess, Artemis.
- A mineral related to lunar energy, such as selenite, moonstone, or any clear, white or silver stone you feel called to.
- A white or silver candle.
- A small bag (cloth or organza is lovely for this, but truly anything will do).
- A piece of paper.
- Something to write with.
- String.

On the evening of a new moon, sit somewhere quietly and comfortably, close your eyes and take three deep breaths. With each breath, visualise a glowing circle emanating from your centre and surrounding you.

On the front of the piece of paper write an invocation to Artemis, or any lunar deity you feel connected with. This can be a short letter or poem inviting her (or whatever name you call her/him/them/it) to join you, graciously requesting that she gift you with her guidance and blessings.

Now light the candle – be sure to use a fire-proof holder for your safety – and read your invocation out loud.

Once the candle is lit and the invocation has been read, turn over the piece of paper, and on the back write the new beginning you would like this divine moon entity to help you manifest. Be sure to use the present tense. It can be as specific as: 'I begin writing my book and it is marvellous!' or as broad as: 'I begin a new phase of wellbeing.' Your own words are essential, because the more personal your magic is, the more powerful it becomes.

Now roll up the paper in a little scroll and tie it with the string. Place this in the spell bag along with some mugwort and the lunar stone.

Sleep with this magic bag under your pillow until the moon is full – approximately fourteen nights. When this time period is over, you can then carry the bag with you or place it somewhere for safekeeping, where it will bring you some extra lunar magic whenever you need it and remind you that you and your new commitment are supported by the sky.

Remember: it's important to have good magical manners! When your intention or project feels like it's on a roll, be sure to thank your moon deity for helping you grow and glow ever more brightly, just like they do.

Sonic Meditations
by Pauline Oliveros

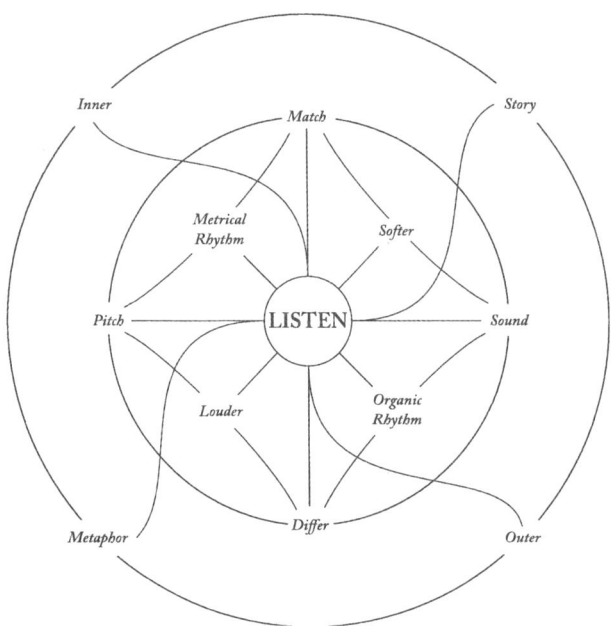

Pauline Oliveros has abandoned composition/performance practice as it is usually established today in favour of Sonic Explorations, which include everyone who wants to participate. She attempts to erase the subject/object or performer/audience relationship by returning to ancient forms that preclude spectators. She is interested in communication among all forms of life, through Sonic Energy. She is especially interested in the healing power of Sonic Energy and its transmission within groups.

Each Sonic Meditation is a special procedure for the following:
1 Actually making sounds.
2 Actively imagining sounds.
3 Listening to present sounds.
4 Remembering sounds.

Healing can occur in relation to the above activities: 1) when individuals feel the common bond with others through a shared experience; 2) when one's inner experience is made manifest and accepted by others; 3) when one is aware of and in tune with one's surroundings; 4) when one's memories, or values, are integrated with the present and understood by others.

In this process, a kind of music occurs naturally. Its beauty is not through intention, but is intrinsic to the effectiveness of its healing power. This may be felt by the group, and the music relates to the people who make it through participation and sharing, as a stream or river whose waters offer refreshment and cleansing to those who find it.

IX The Greeting

Informed persons should begin the greeting at least half an hour or more before a scheduled meeting or program. After you are seated and comfortable, allow a tone to come into mind. Keep returning your attention to this same tone. Everytime a person or persons enter this space, greet them by singing the tone as you were greeted when you entered this space. Continue this meditation until all are present.

X Have you ever heard the sound of an iceberg melting?

Begin this meditation with the greeting meditation (IX). At the designated time for all persons to be present, begin an eight to fifteen minute imperceptible dimming of the house lights, down to as dark as possible. When the lights are about halfway down, begin a flood of white noise at the threshold of audibility. Slowly make an imperceptible crescendo to a predetermined sound level safe for human ears. Approximately twenty minutes later, introduce one brilliant light flash. After an hour from the beginning has passed, begin projections on the walls of colourful mandalas, patterns resembling the aurora borealis, or simply colours of the spectrum. The light intensity of these projections should be no greater than the threshold of visibility, or just noticeable. These may continue for approximately thirty minutes. Thirty minutes before the white noise ends the space should be illuminated by white light, slowly over about eight minutes, from the threshold of visibility to as brilliant as possible. The brilliance must exceed normal house lighting and approach the intensity of daylight. The end of the light and sound should be sudden and synchronous. Darkness and silence should be maintained for ten minutes or more, then illuminate the space with dim blue light for continued meditation in silence and finally exit of the participants. The duration of this meditation is approximately two to four hours or more. All adjustments of light and sound intensity should be pre-set and preferably voltage controlled, so that all present may participate in the meditation and that activities extraneous to meditation may be avoided. Participants must be comfortable either sitting or lying down.

Variation: If multiple speakers are used for the production of white noise, one or two persons per speaker could perform meditation movements such as tai chi in front of the speakers, at a distance of two to four feet, thus creating sound shadows. The sound shadows could gradually be complemented by visible shadows activated by just noticeable light sources. The duration of this part of the meditation could be approximately thirty to forty minutes and succeed or overlap the just noticeable projected images.

XIX

Lie flat on your back or sit comfortably. Open your eyes widely, then let your eyelids close extremely slowly. Become aware of how your eyelids are closing. When your eyelids are closed, turn your eyes slowly from left to right, around, up and down. Let your eyes rest comfortably in their sockets. Try to be aware of the muscles behind the eyes and of the distance from these muscles to the back of the head. Cover your eyes with your palms and shut out all the light. Become aware of all the sounds in the environment. When you think you have established contact with all of the sounds in the external environment, very gradually, introduce your fingers into your ears or cover them with your palms. Try to shut out all external sound. Listen carefully to the internal sounds of your own body working. After a long time, gradually open your ears and include the sounds of the external environment.

XX Your Voice

Think of the sound of your own voice. What is its fundamental pitch? What is its range? What is its quality? What does it express, no matter what you might be verbalising or singing? What was the original sound of your voice before you learned to sound the way you sound now?

Excerpted from *Sonic Meditations* by Pauline Oliveros, by permission of Pauline Oliveros Productions and Ministry of Maat, Inc. © 2021.

Acupressure
by Maria Christofi

Acupuncture is an ancient form of healing believed by many to originate in China. In Chinese medicine, *qi* – life-energy – flows through the body along a network of channels called meridians. Various acupuncture points placed along the meridians act like stations or gateways where you can stimulate the qi and free up energy and blood flow. The saying "where qi flows, blood follows" illustrates the importance of the free flow of qi and blood in the body to enhance the health of internal organs and prevent stagnation.

Acupressure is a way of stimulating these acupuncture points without using needles, making it an easy way to incorporate the benefits of Chinese traditional medicine into your self-care routines. Here I've selected my top ten priority points for general health for most people every day.

Using gentle yet firm pressure with either your middle finger or thumb, massage the points in a circular motion for about ten seconds, breathe deeply and bring your attention to the circulation of qi. Making a deep connection with the point is easier if you massage the whole vicinity around the point first. This warms the area and gets the blood circulating to enliven that point.

Just a few minutes of pressure on these key points unblocks your meridians, helping to reset your body's subtle energy layers. As you press, your brain releases endorphins, alleviating pain and encouraging tension to recede so that blood flows more freely.

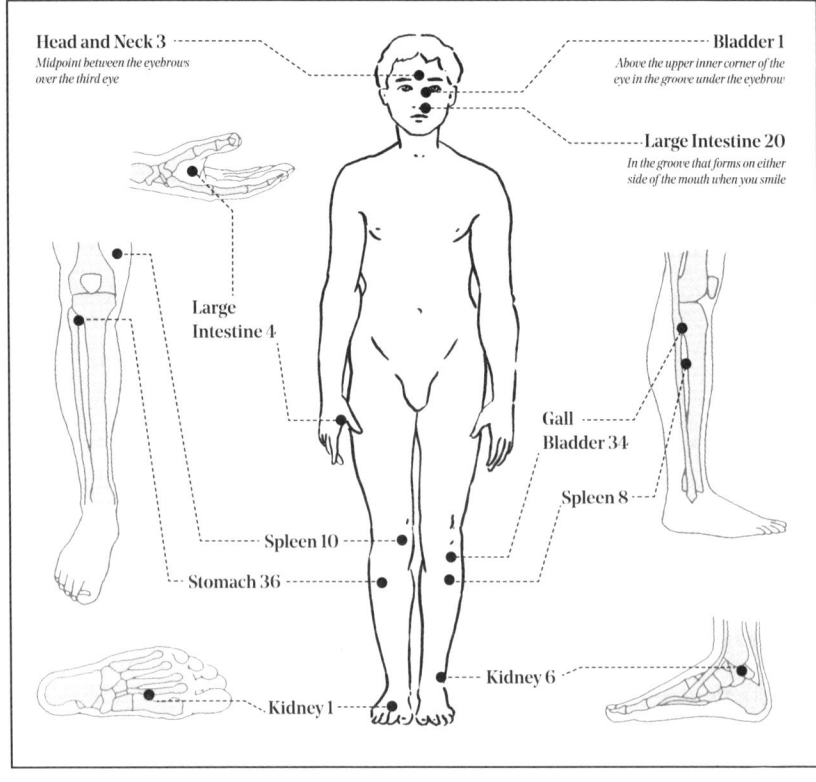

Head and Neck 3 — *Midpoint between the eyebrows over the third eye*

Bladder 1 — *Above the upper inner corner of the eye in the groove under the eyebrow*

Large Intestine 20 — *In the groove that forms on either side of the mouth when you smile*

Large Intestine 4

Gall Bladder 34

Spleen 8

Spleen 10

Stomach 36

Kidney 6

Kidney 1

Stomach 36
Zusanli
Leg Three Miles

Out of all of the points I've chosen here, this is the most important point to massage daily for its immune-boosting properties and general contribution to health and longevity. Ancient texts describe how this point was was used on soldiers to keep them going an extra few miles. One of the most commonly used points in Chinese traditional medicine, Leg Three Miles is helpful for the treatment of all manner of digestive issues, menstrual disorders, and any muscular issues in the legs. It's also thought to calm the spirit and generally nourish the qi, blood and overall health.

Location: About three thumb-widths down from the knee, about one cm from the tibia bone.

→ Fatigue
→ Many digestive conditions including nausea, vomiting, reflux, stomach cramps, bloating, flatulence, diarrhoea, low appetite and poor digestion
→ Strengthens the immune system
→ Calms the spirit
→ Menstrual issues such as period pain

Kidney 6
Zhaohai
Shining Sea

A key point in the treatment of fatigue, Shining Sea is a very grounding and relaxing point that is helpful for sleep issues, stress and anxiety. I often use it at the end of my treatments along with Kidney 1 and Bladder 25. It is also often used for menstrual issues such as period pain, or when a pregnant person is having a difficult labour. As the kidney channel passes through the throat, Shining Sea is also a good one to stimulate for sore throats.

Location: Shining Sea is a thumb-width below the inner ankle in a depression between the tendons. It may become easier to find if you massage the whole area.

→ Regulates menstruation
→ Nourishes the body
→ Urinary issues
→ Insomnia
→ Calms the spirit

Spleen 10
Xuehai
Sea of Blood

A major point in the treatment of menstrual and gynaecological issues, hence the name. In Chinese medicine, what we call 'blood stagnation' is normally at the root of most menstrual issues. The key function of Sea of Blood is to treat sluggish blood circulation; it can often contract quite deeply when needled which really gets the blood flowing.

Location: Located over the quadriceps muscle, cup your right palm to the left knee with the thumb facing into the centre of the body. The point is about one inch above where your thumb rests. Will feel warm when activated.

→ Menstrual issues such as painful or irregular periods
→ Endometriosis, fibroids
→ Anaemia
→ Leg pain
→ Urinary issues
→ Nourishing blood after birth

Large Intestine 4
Hegu
Joining Valley

One of the most powerful points for treating qi and blood circulation, it is contraindicated for use during pregnancy. It's a good point to bring on menstruation in the case of delayed or missing periods, and for use for any pain in the body. It's also thought to regulate the mouth, ears, nose and eyes, making it an effective point for respiratory issues.

Location: The best way to stimulate Joining Valley is to hold your thumb on the palm side and the index finger on top of the web between the thumb and index finger. Pinch and hold. It's very strong so it will be easy to find.

→ Induces labour
→ Lack of periods or delayed periods
→ Pain relief
→ Headache
→ Nasal congestion
→ Nosebleed
→ Hayfever
→ Colds and fever

Kidney 1
Yongquan
Bubbling Spring

Bubbling Spring is the lowest acupressure point of the body and is considered to be very grounding – imagining roots descending from this point and stimulating with acupressure can have a nurturing and stabilising effect. As the first point on the kidney channel, which relates to the water element, Bubbling Spring is seen as the entry point of the water element of the body, hence the name.

The kidney energy of the body is often low during winter so this is a good point to start pressing when the nights get longer. An old text called *The Song of the Nine Needles for Returning the Yang* states that this point "returns the yang", meaning that it warms and nourishes when excess cold has entered the body. It's well stimulated by a hot foot soak, making it a good place to start a regular self-care ritual. Another way to stimulate this point is to place a golf ball on the floor and roll your foot over it.

Location: Located over the quadriceps muscle, cup your right palm to the left knee with the thumb facing into the centre of the body. The point is about one inch above where your thumb rests. Will feel warm when activated.

→ Menstrual issues such as painful or irregular periods
→ Endometriosis, fibroids
→ Anaemia
→ Leg pain
→ Urinary issues
→ Nourishing blood after birth

Gall Bladder 34
Yanglingquan
Yang Mound Spring

A key point for stress, studies have shown that stimulating Yang Mound Spring increases the concentration of gamma-aminobutyric acid (GABA) in the body, which helps to relieve spasm and decrease tension. Yang Mound Spring circulates qi so use when feeling sluggish to clear stagnation in the tendons. The gallbladder is also related to creativity so massage this point to free up creative flow or when feeling stuck.

Location: Slide your hand up the outside of the lower leg until the flesh becomes bone – this is the head of the fibula. From the head of the fibula measure down one thumb-width and then across one thumb-width towards the front of the leg. This point will feel quite tender and you will definitely find it if you massage all the tissue in the area that feels tight.

→ Tension headache
→ Leg and joint issues
→ Stress and anxiety
→ Neck and shoulder pain
→ Menstrual issues such as period pain

Large Intestine 20
Yingxiang
Welcome Fragrance

As its name suggests, this point stimulates our ability to breathe and smell, making it the most significant local point for nasal conditions. Incorporate this point into facial massage routines to keep the nasal passages clear. Even more effective after a steam inhalation if you're suffering from a cold or hayfever or any sort of nasal congestion. Stimulate this point with your index fingers. Resting your elbows on your lap or a table will create more pressure as you lean forward onto your fingers.

Location: You will find this point in the groove that forms on either side of the mouth when you smile. It is level with the mid-point of the outside of the nostril.

→ Nasal issues such as congestion, loss of sense of smell, hayfever
→ Sinusitis

Bladder 1
Jingming
Bright Eyes

Rarely needled in acupuncture practice due to its very close location to the eye. Relieves many externally caused disorders of the eye, such as dryness or irritation from the wind, eye tension from headaches and eye strain from computer screens. Rest your elbows on the table or your lap with your index fingers placed in the points, then lean your head onto your fingers at the depth that feels right.

Location: Above the upper inner corner of the eye in the groove under the eyebrow. It has a very soothing effect so you will know when you find it.

→ Headache
→ Eye strain, irritation

Spleen 8
Diji
Earth Pivot

Massaging all along the inner aspect of the leg including this point is very soothing if experiencing period or leg pain. Regular work on this will soften the tissue and make for more efficient blood circulation in the lower leg.

Location: Find your way from the inner side of the knee and keep feeling down the leg until you you fall into a soft depression after the knee bone. Then measure down three thumb-widths. This point is just next to the tibia bone.

→ Menstrual issues such as painful or irregular periods
→ Leg pain
→ Any sort of pelvic pain
→ Digestive issues

Extra Points: Head and Neck 3
Yintang
Hall of Impression

The most widely requested acupuncture point in my treatment room, Hall of Impression has calming and meditative qualities. It may feel like there's a hole between the eyebrows when this point is activated; you may become aware of the energy body 'breathing' in and out of this point.

Location: At the midpoint between the eyebrows over the third eye.

→ Insomnia
→ Anxiety
→ Stress
→ Frontal headache
→ Hay fever
→ Sinus issues such as sinusitis and nasal congestion

Ayurveda and Prajna
by Mira Manek

When I hit my lowest point some years ago, not knowing what was happening in my life and unable to rise from that deep, hollow, sinking feeling, I started to think of only the day ahead. I realised that by taking each day one at a time, doing things in that day that I knew made me happy – whether it was sitting in the sun, going for a yoga or spin class, meeting a friend – I could guarantee at least a few moments of happiness. This carried me through the year, fuelling my day with moments and things that I knew would lift me. What I realise now is that over time, I created a toolkit of rituals to help me survive. Now this toolkit has grown, I've delved deeper into my practices and found new ones. It is no longer just a toolkit for survival, but one with which to truly thrive.

A lot of the practices and rituals I write about in my book *Prajna* are based on the principles of Ayurveda, and are things that you can weave into your life and create your own playlist from. To be well and happy, we need to feel this both in body and mind. Each is as important as the other, and thus my book delves into movement, food, philosophy and spirituality.

Why Prajna

Prajna is intuitive wisdom. It is beyond the realm of knowledge and intellect. It is accessed from stillness and is akin to the concept of *shunyata*: nothingness, emptiness, where thoughts and events of the mind are observed and noted without any connection to stories or experience, without any presuppositions, not connecting a past occurrence with the present moment, but just living here. Prajna is echoed in the concept in Zen Buddhism called *mushin* which literally means "mind without mind" or mindlessness, a mind that is in fact entirely present, a mind free from worry, free from anger and fear, a mind that is truly mindful. Prajna, therefore, is perceiving the vastness of void, living with absolute freedom, living in the present moment. It is the realisation that we do not need to strive for *moksha* or liberation once we leave this earth, but that living in this bliss of presentness, of mindfulness and awareness, this itself is liberation.

Ayurveda

Ayurveda, a Sanskrit word meaning 'life health' or 'life science', is the basis of traditional holistic medicine in India. It is in fact a scripture, a Veda, written in Sanskrit, whose teachings are as relevant today as they were thousands of years ago. The British closed all Ayurvedic colleges in India during their Raj in 1833 so that only Western medicine was to be practised. It is incredible now to see such a revival of this ancient science that this book is being published in London.

Ayurveda is one of the world's oldest medical systems, developed by ancient seers and natural scientists. It is a way of life based on balance: when you eat is just as important as what you eat and how much you eat, movement and yoga go hand in hand with food, and keeping the mind at ease and not allowing for stress is an essential part of the package. Thus, it is a lifestyle comprising of and connecting the elements of mind, body and spirit, a lifestyle that is wholesome, pure and nourishing, one that is *sattvic*, eating foods that are also sattvic, for it is said in the ancient scripture of *The Upanishads* that food is Brahman, the higher consciousness, the true self, the Divine.

Prakruti, our constitution

Ayurvedic medicine is based on balance and harmony. Our wellness and happiness depend on living in harmony with our environment and achieving an internal balance between opposing forces or energies. First there are the three fundamental bodily energies, or *doshas*. These are *vata*, which is characterised by the mobile nature of wind energy; *pitta*, which embodies transformative fire energy; and *kapha*, which reflects the binding nature of water and earth energy. We are made up of these doshas and the balance of the three in our body determine our physical and emotional constitution. It is this that determines what we should and should not be eating, how our energy levels rise and fall through the day and change according to season. An Ayurvedic practitioner or *vaidya* can determine this accurately, assess which elements are in balance and which are out, and then diagnose according to this. By implementing certain practices and changes, we can bring about a better balance within our dosha constitution. It is this balance that, in Ayurveda, is the key to good health.

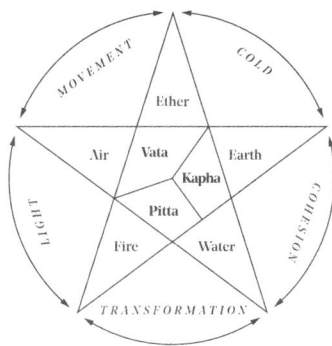

Connecting to nature
Our bodies and minds are instinctively attuned to nature. We may have lost that over time through our busy lives with a myriad of distractions, diversions and temptations. Ayurveda is a way to find this connection again, a back-to-basics approach to life at the centre of which is self-awareness. The practice of meditation is to bring about this very thing – a sense of self, understanding the inner voice, listening to our body, connecting with nature. And being present is key to this, thus we find ourselves at the origin of mindfulness.

The Ayurvedic perspective that humans came from nature is echoed in the words of Alan Watts, "You didn't come into this world. You came out of it, like a wave from the ocean." We must find a way to bridge the gap between the ancient and modern, a way to connect with our roots and, like a tree, grow those roots and be stable in ourselves, so that we stand tall and remain grounded through the intense storms and blistering sunshine of life. The answer to health and healing is in the balance of the senses and the elements, both in our body and mind and in the universe.

Agni, the digestive fire
In India, during spiritual and Vedic rituals, a *havan*, *yagna* or spiritual fire is made and *ahuti* or oblations are offered into the fire while mantras are chanted. The fire absorbs and takes what it needs in order to burn brighter and eliminates the rest. In the same way, our digestive fire is kindled with cooked foods, our body assimilates the nutrients it needs and eliminates what it does not need. Eating cooked foods, drinking warm to hot water, fasting between meals and yoga and *pranayama* all help to stimulate the *agni*. Having a good digestive system, a fire that is well-fed, we produce a biochemical or subtle force called *ojas*. This is the fruit of our digestion, the inner glow, the vigour of mind and the essence of immunity.

Dosha	Elements	Characteristics	Attributes in Balance	Attributes when Unbalanced
Vata	Aether & Air	Lean, light frame, dry hair and cold hands and feet	Agile and energetic, excited by new experiences, inspirational and creative	Insomnia, irregularity in energy levels, appetite and mood
Pitta	Fire & Water	Well proportioned muscular frame and moist blemish-prone skin	Abundant energy, strong metabolism, determined and focused. Sleeping soundly for short periods of time	Excessive heat, indigestion, aggressive or argumentative
Kapha	Earth & Water	Larger frame, thick hair and soft smooth skin	Loyal, naturally calm and emotionally supportive, sound heavy sleep and regular digestion	Increase in weight and chronic fatigue, stubborn

Dreamwork: Active Imagination
by Jennifer Dumpert

Different sleep stages produce different kinds of dreams. The dream states of hypnagogia (during the onset of sleep) and hypnopompia (leading out of sleep), which together make up liminal dreaming, exist at the boundaries of sleep and waking states. If you devote yourself to exploring the dream space at the edges of consciousness, you become a consciousness explorer and your world expands.

The word 'liminal' comes from the Latin word *limen*, which means threshold or doorway, the in-between that joins places. Liminal dreams are those that come in the middle zones, between sleep and waking. When you lie down at night or coast up to consciousness in the morning, you can think of that final state as your goal. But you can also abide in the space in between, a transitional zone at the edge of consciousness that can become its own goal. It's a remarkable place.

Practices are a form of evocation, a way to summon what most matters into your life. This is really a very simple equation: doing something regularly brings its object more regularly into your experience. The first, crucial component for starting your own dream practice is a diary or a journal to record your dreams – through writing, drawing, collages or music. Choose any method that requires you to pay attention and to devote energy to the pursuit.

Liminal dreaming is easier to learn than lucid dreaming, while also providing cognitive liberty – the freedom to experience and explore your consciousness on your own terms. Because liminal dream states provide access to your daytime self while freeing your mind from the dictates of the waking world, the opportunity for therapeutic exploration is great. They can also be harnessed for endeavors of the rational mind. Myriad examples exist of scientists, artists, and writers tapping into the power of liminal dreaming for creativity, even to solve scientific problems.

Most of the time you spend in liminal dream states, you retain at least some semblance of your waking self. The logical, linear and focused part of your mind remains active to varying degrees. But you're also dreaming, adrift among intuitive, visual, emotional thought processes and associations. When liminal dreaming, you're utilising the concrete reasoning of the waking world while also moving through an unreal place of possibility: you move simultaneously through the world we all share and one of your mind's own making.

Aristotle suggests that our dreaming consciousness is structured by memory and on what the senses perceive when we're awake. Memory is a collection of stored duplicates that we create from what we see, hear, smell, touch and taste. But memory isn't the only faculty we use to construct this alternative, interior world. Imagination also comes into play. Imagination is not only the basis of creativity, but a way of perceiving the world.

Carl Jung is one of many thinkers who considered imagination an organ of perception and understanding. His idea of 'active imagination' can provide a basis for the process of leading people into hypnagogia in order to bridge the conscious and unconscious. As the name implies, active imagination also helps us understand the imagination as a faculty of perception.

Jung thought that active imagination allowed the conscious mind to directly perceive what normally remained hidden. By teaching the practice of active imagination, Jung felt he could help patients watch their minds work, and bring those workings to life through the creative engagement and expression of what they discovered there.

But for Jung this surfacing was only the beginning of what he considered to be the two main phases of active imagination. The second part of the process arose after the creative expression. In this phase, the ego steps forward and takes the lead. Utilising reason, the practitioner evaluates everything from part one and slowly and sometimes painfully integrates it into daily experience. Jung strongly believed that learning to understand and communicate with the unconscious, and to then bring what we learn into full awareness, naturally resolved many psychological issues.

During his own early forays into active imagination, Jung recorded his experiences in a series of journals, initially called his 'black books.' He then commissioned the creation of a red leather book with blank pages that he gradually filled with beautiful calligraphy and art. Long hidden in the hands of the Jung family, this private volume was released as *The Red Book*. Jung called the wild times when he created these powerful images the most important of his life, and the prima materia for his lifelong work.

Though he taught patients how to do it, he also insisted people could do it spontaneously. He called it both a technique and a process. The same can be said of liminal dreaming in general. One can learn how to do it and purposefully seek the benefits, but it also just happens without any work or intervention. Liminal dreaming clearly lends itself well to active imagination in allowing symbols, images, ideas and other languages of the unconscious to surface into conscious understanding.

The active imagination exercise I offer here is a combination of Jung's and von Franz's classic processes with Robert A. Johnson's more recent method, which he describes in his 1986 book *Inner Work: Using Dreams and Active Imagination for Personal Growth*.

Active Imagination

1. Set the scene for the creative process. Keep something handy nearby, like a notebook or sketchpad, clay, etc.
2. Get yourself into a liminal dream state. This is the Dalí/Edison method for hypnagogia, so called after Salvador, the Spanish surrealist artist, and the American inventor Thomas Edison, who conceived more or less the same exercise independently of each other.
    a. Sit comfortably in a chair. If you're at work, try this at your desk. You can also recline. If you really can't nap, even lightly, sitting up, go ahead and lie down.
    b. Hold onto something that will clatter loudly when you drop it. You can try holding something over metal plates. You can also hold a bell, a handful of coins, or a jingly dog toy. If you're lying down, just raise your arm in the air.
    c. Keep something next to you to record what arises.
    d. Drift off into hypnagogia.
    e. Once you drop what you're holding, or your arm drops, without doing anything else start capturing what's in your mind.
3. Sink into the flow of the liminal dream state with the intention of encountering meaningful symbols, images, ideas or impulses. Do not attempt to control or manipulate the experience, but don't allow yourself to simply drift into fantasising. Watch what arises with the idea that your unconscious can communicate and teach you about the contents of your mind.
4. Once something intriguing appears, or as soon as you begin to transition out of the liminal dream state, begin the process of giving form or expression to whatever stood out. Start a drawing, record yourself singing or dancing — whatever helps bring the gifts of the unconscious into waking life.
5. Allow the creative process to become a meditation. As you write or paint, think about what you perceived and why it felt important to you. Ask yourself what message your unconscious has for you.
6. As you continue to engage with your creative process, you may want to re-enter the liminal dream state to refresh whatever it was that caught your attention. Do not hurry. Allow the process to take however long it takes, whether that's hours, days or months.

Restoration Ecology
by Elias Haase

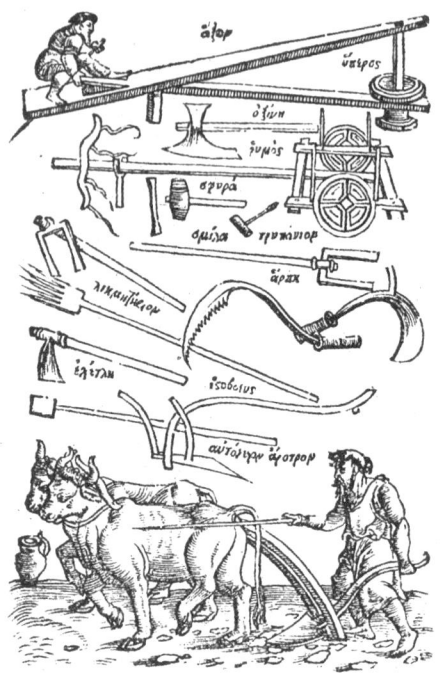

Image: Greek farming woodcut by Conrad Gessner, 1560.

I started my regenerative farm in the foothills of the Montseny national park in Catalunya a few years ago, but the journey to get here has been much longer. Along the way I was inspired by many people and many small ideas that added up to where I am today: overlooking a no-dig market garden, fields of spelt for beer, a mobile chicken coop for rotational pasturing and the beginnings of many other projects.

In my contribution to this year's calendar I want to leave as many crumbs of inspiration as possible. A theme for every month, things to try and sense. You will also find selections from the French Republican calendar, an attempt to create a secular, nature dictated calendar that was used during the first Republic and by the Paris Commune. Each day of the year celebrates something in nature or farming. I find it useful to find different inspiration every day.

But before you move on to the day-to-day of the year, let's take a moment to discuss regenerative farming and restoration ecology.

Modern human activity over the past 400 years has led to severe degradation of the ecosystems we inhabit and are part of. 'Restoration ecology' is an umbrella term that covers all methods, new and ancient, that are being used to help ecosystems recover. Permaculture, Holistic Management, rotational grazing, no-till farming, sustainable forestry, rewilding, reintroduction of native species and a myriad of other disciplines are all facets of the holistic approach to restoration ecology.

Restoration ecology is not just about how we can 'manage' nature better. It is also about us as humans, our inner world and our history. Those of us who have been reared on the stories of Western supremacy and solutionism need to learn to think on a smaller scale. The ideas that might save our sphere have been with us, around us for as long as humans have made tools. These ideas can flourish if we give them space, and if we listen to the guidance of Indigenous groups who have preserved and lived the very ideas that will save the world. 80% of global biodiversity is stewarded by Indigenous people, and forests guarded by Indigenous people are the most resistant and show the lowest levels of decline.

The ideas are there, the experts exist and are fighting. I suggest that this year could be about listening, following and thinking small.

If there is an element you want to get to know more this year, make it soil. The keys to our future may very well be hidden among the crumbles. We are losing topsoil at a rate ten times faster than we can replenish it. When European colonisers started the agricultural exploitation of the Great Plains in North America, soil fertility plummeted more than 70% in thirty years. Soil is an incredible meta-organism of bacteria, fungi, yeasts, plants and animals. The past decades have seen a greater understanding of the importance of soil, along with different approaches. Cover-cropping, no-till farming, Holistic Management and more have emerged and are slowly changing farming. When stewarded right, soil can absorb astonishing amounts of carbon while nourishing the lushest plants. Soil building and restoration can be done nearly anywhere. Establish a no-till garden on your front lawn. Implement holistic grazing on a field you own or lease. Establish gorilla leaf compost in public spaces.

This year, take the steps towards the land you have been thinking about. Hike and observe. Sleep outside in a rainstorm. Walk further than you've ever walked. Grow tomatoes and make compost. Plant chestnut trees. Be out there, be in here.

January

More activity than you might think. Have a look around, see how many species of bird you can identify. Look for tracks in the snow or the mud.

Now is a great time to dream about your plans for this year. Work backwards. What do I want to grow and for whom? For yourself or for the foodbank? For a village or just one person? If you need help finding your way, consider writing a holistic goal with everyone who will be involved. The **holistic goal** is part of the toolkit of Holistic Management, an approach to restoration ecology and sustainable grazing – there are many templates and examples available online.

The landscape looks lifeless but there are a few of our plant cousins who like to get started at this time. Peas and a few bean varieties love getting sown outdoors now. Indoor sowing of the impatient varieties is getting underway.

In the Republican Calendar 1 January, or 12 Nivôse, celebrates **clay**.

February

Winter is coming to an end. Watch for the first shoots poking through. Smell the air and hear the quality of sounds. The squelch of mud and the crunch of freshly frozen snow.

If you are establishing a vegetable garden of any size, now is the time to get your ducks in a row. Indoor sowing picks up. Get your beds in order. Turn your attention to fruit and nut trees. Time to prune.

You will still have a bit of time to plan and sow the first trays, the season has not started in earnest. Read about soil and identify the types you are working with in your garden, field or yard. Fill half a glass jar with your soil. Add water to the brim and shake thoroughly. Leave the jar alone for a day.

You will be able to identify distinct layers of sand, clay and organic material.

In the Republican Calendar 14 February, or 26 Pluviôse, celebrates **woad**.

March

After the last heavy frost has passed, you might be able to start planting trees in some places. In Catalunya, now is the time to establish new vineyards. March is the time for rooting, preparing for later bursts of foliage.

If using chickens in your rotational grazing, you will probably establish new flocks now. Existing flocks will start laying.

You may see the last frost this month, and so the work starts in earnest. Transplanting and direct sowing is in full swing.

In Southern Europe the wild asparagus season starts and the hills are crawling with foragers.

In the Republican Calendar 11 March, or 21 Ventôse, celebrates **mandrake**.

April

Great hiking and foraging weather. Enjoy hiding from a shower under a tree. Everything is beginning to flower. A month of opportunity and risk. A good April will make your season, a bad one may ruin you. Nothing to be done except to wait and hope.

The bees are emerging from their hibernation and the queen starts laying eggs. Foragers are collecting the first nectar. Species like the Asian hornet *(vespa velutina)*, are establishing new nests.

If you have established a storage pond or tank, April is a crucial month. How much water can be saved for a long, dry summer?

In the Republican Calendar 21 April, or 2 Floréal, celebrates the **oak**.

May

Make May the month to think about grain. Bred over thousands of generations from different varieties of wild grass: rice, corn, wheat, spelt, kamut, millet, sorghum, barley. These are the basis for tortillas, beer, pasta and bread.

When you pass a grain field, see if you can already see kernels forming. Are the kernels milky or doughy inside? That tells you about the stage of maturity. Milky before doughy before hard.

Almost all modern grain varieties are annual. Every year they need to be sown anew. Usually this involves tillage, fertiliser and a whole lot of topsoil loss. But the interaction between humans and plants has never stopped and not all new developments are GMO. Over the past decades The Land Institute has been breeding a particular type of wheatgrass *(thinopyrum intermedium)* to produce bigger kernels. The past few years have seen the first larger successful trials of the perennial grain. Perennial grain!

If you want to learn more about sustainable grain production look up the work of Masanobu Fukuoka, The Land Institute and the native corn varieties of the Americas.

In the Republican Calendar 26 May, or 7 Prairial, celebrates **oat grass**.

June

This month, focus on the movement of the sun. Where does it rise? How does it move across the sky? Feel the heat on your face.

June brings forth many greens. Lettuce, spinach, marigold, mustard and more. Just think how much careful stewardship went into the transformation of the bitter, rubbery wild ancestors to the sweet and tender lettuce or spinach.

Think about the relationship of our garden crops to their ancestors. Lettuce, for example, has calming and pain relieving effects. Less so than its wild cousin, but the sap looks similar and the effect is there. Does that change the way you think about lettuce?

In the Republican Calendar 6 June, or 18 Prairial, celebrates the **poppy**.

July

If all has gone well this might be the month of the grain harvest. Blades and stalks wilt and the kernels dry out. For the grain to be storable long term the moisture content of the kernels must be below 16%. Modern farmers use electronic moisture sensors but you can replicate a very simple moisture test at home. Collect a small sample of kernels in a glass jar and add fine salt. If the salt sticks to the kernels they are still too moist. If the kernels and the salt separate easily, harvest can commence.

On the other end of the dry-wet spectrum we find the tomato. Juicy, sweet and plentiful around this time of year. Tomatoes have become an important part of cuisines all over the world, but before 1492 the plant could have only been found in South America. When you eat a tomato, think of the Indigenous people of Central America who probably first domesticated its wild nightshade ancestor.

In the Republican Calendar the 19 July, or 1 Thermidor, celebrates **spelt**.

August

Depending on the year this month is probably dusty and dry. Cover crops, mulching and deep-compost gardening are designed to reduce evaporation and soil loss through wind in this period.

But the forests are dry, and fire season is afoot in many areas. On some days the world seems to stand still. The quality of sound changes.

Fire management is an important part of modern life in an increasing number of places. Indigenous people all over the world have practiced ritual burning as a way to clear combustible material from the forest before too much accumulates for tens of thousands of years. Large fires as we are seeing now are the result of modern farming and forestry practices, as well as climate change. We have eliminated animals that are part of a healthy fire forest and stopped ritual burning practices, which have been made illegal in most places.

The restoration of our forests must include the reintroduction of animals like bison, which keep the undergrowth in check, as well as the practising of ritual burns.

Another keystone animal for the restoration of drought-stricken ecosystems in the Northern Hemisphere is the beaver. Beavers slow the flow of water and create storage ponds and ecosystems for plants and animals. Over the past century they were largely driven to extinction, but recently reintroduced in the UK and other countries.

In the Republican Calendar the 20 August, or 3 Fructidor, celebrates the **puffball mushroom**.

September

September brings relief in much of the Northern Hemisphere. Lower temperatures and rain return in many places. This is a good time to think about being subject to weather. Much of modern life happens insulated from the weather. Most activities are not impacted much by weather patterns. Imagine you didn't have water until the rains returned. No cool spaces until temperatures dropped.

In the Republican Calendar the 24 September, or 3 Vendémiaire, celebrates the **chestnut**.

October

Cold mornings, rainy days. Speaking of rain, which watershed do you live in? How does rainwater flow around you? Where does it pool and where does it drain?

In permaculture the flow of water across a piece of land is a key pillar of your overall design. Spend a few rainy days exploring the land around you, city or countryside, and familiarise yourself with the journey of water from the highest to the lowest points.

Depending on where you live now is the time to sow grains with longer growth cycles, like spelt. The plant germinates quickly and will deepen its root network over the winter months, to emerge vigorously in spring and be harvested in summer.

Grains store energy for the growth of the seedling in the form of starches. As the seed germinates, it produces enzymes that convert starches into sugars. This same process has been used by humans for thousands of years to make beer and malt drinks. Making your own malt and brewing a simple sour beer is not as complicated as you might think.

In the Republican Calendar 12 October, or 21 Vendémiaire, celebrates **hemp**.

November

Now is the time to think about next year's garden. If you haven't yet, think about establishing a no-dig garden with deep mulching. No-dig gardens retain more moisture, preserve mycelial networks and naturally suppress weeds.

Establishing a no-dig garden bed:

- Lay out cardboard in the area you want to convert to no-dig.
- Add 20cm of rich compost on top of the cardboard. Composted manure is preferable. Wood or mushroom compost will do, but might need amendments in spring.
- If possible, cover the beds with a tarp.

In spring your beds will be ready for sowing and planting.

If you want to learn more about no-dig gardening, read *No Dig Organic Home and Garden* by Stephany Hafferty and Charles Dowding.

In the Republican Calendar 29 November, or 9 Frimaire, celebrates the **juniper**.

December

Rest. Enjoy walks, snow, silence, storms, ice, frost.

In the Republican Calendar 2 December, or 14 Frimaire, celebrates **horseradish**.

Open Prayer Protocol
by K Allado-McDowell

What Is Prayer?

Anything can be a prayer: words, thoughts, gestures, songs, gatherings, movement, perceptions. Prayers work in part by creating bridges between interior and exterior, connecting us with ancestors, spirits and the greater universe. They also work through repetition: prayers can be performed at regular intervals (in the morning and at night, for example), as needed when facing the challenges of life or in appreciation of life's blessings. All that is needed to pray is gratitude, an intention, a structure and one's own consciousness.

Belief systems enable prayer by constructing an imaginal cosmos through which we interface with spirit. In postmodern cultures, we are encouraged to construct our own belief systems and practices for accessing the divine. While this situation demands much of our creativity, it also frees us to find what works for us and to develop our own unique approach to spiritual practice. As we do this, we may compare notes, and work together to shape collective practices.

What follows is an open prayer protocol I developed within my own practice and spiritual community, for the purpose of seeking the aid of spirits and ancestors. Following the ethos of open-source software and protocol development, I offer it here for your use and adaptation.

How I Learned the Prayer

On the advice of a Reiki healer, I started constructing a shrine to my ancestors in my small meditation area. I unearthed photos and stories from digital family archives. I printed the photos and arranged them next to my mesa alongside rattles, plant tinctures and other power objects.

When I sat down to meditate, I prayed with tobacco and a plant called *tsunu* (known by Western botanists as *Platycyamus regnelli*) holding these in my hands or ingesting them. The tsunu tree is known for the spiritually cleansing properties of its bark, for its regenerative properties in woodland restoration, and for its resilience to drought and stony soil. Tobacco is the gatekeeper and diplomat. In contemplation with these allies, I reached out to the spirit world, and was shown a way to pray.

As I prayed, I met ancestors. They showed me that we could work together. As an incarnate being in the physical world, connected to them through history, matter and information, I could work on their behalf, and they, in turn, would work with me from their home in the spirit world. As I deepened my prayer practice, these worlds knitted together and a protocol emerged: a system for prayer made through trial and error. Over years, I refined this protocol.

Prayers are seeds. If you nourish them with your life they will grow and healing will happen. Repetition and focus are necessary for prayer to bear fruit. Routine and ritual use the body's memory to focus the mind, preparing the ground in which prayers are planted. In this organic model of growth each step forward is followed by integration and consolidation, producing a solid structure that can be shared with others.

Below are instructions for making the prayer. This can be done individually or in a group. In fact, I used this protocol with a monthly new moon prayer circle over Zoom during the quarantine periods of 2020.

The Prayer

Establish a calm and meditative mind through ritual actions like lighting a candle and adopting a prayerful posture. Speak this prayer out loud, adapting its contents to correspond with your own specific allies, medicines, and relationships. Sometimes I visualise a field of white light before me, speaking the prayer into the heart network of infinitely expanding love.

(Optional musical marker: a bell, bowl, or gong, or a sung AUM)
Thank you ancestors.
Thank you ancestors of my mother. (Visualise ancestors.)
Thank you ancestors of my father. (Visualise ancestors.)
Thank you ancestral spirits of the land.
Thank you ancestral wisdom-keepers of my practice.
Thank you primordial ancestor.
Thank you Earth spirits (such as Apus and Nagas).
Thank you Great Spirit, Divine Mother, God, etc. for this life and for this path.
Thank you for Pachamama, Earth, Gaia, etc. and all of her medicines.

(Thank your medicine allies.)
For example:
Thank you for Grandmother Ayahuasca and Chacruna.
Thank you for Grandfather Huachuma and Grandfather Tobacco.
Thank you for Uña de Gato.
Thank you for Camalonga.
Etc.
(Thank your personal animal spirit helpers, visualising yourself taking on their forms and characteristics.)
For example:
Thank you Spider.
Thank you Jaguar.
Thank you Condor.
Etc.

***

Thank you for my Mother and Father Great Spirit.
Thank you for my siblings and their partner(s) and children.
Thank you for my partner(s) and my children and animal companions.
Thank you for my teachers (name teachers), and their teachers, and their teachers.
Thank you for my spiritual community.
Please guide us and protect us and enable us to do our work.
Great Spirit, I ask that you purify me so I may fulfill the role destined for me.
I ask that you grant me Wisdom, Strength, and Clarity of Mind, Great Spirit.
I ask that you illuminate my path so that I may always walk in the Light.
Please bless my words.
Please bless my actions.
Please bless the music of my life.
Affirmation (For example: Aho, Amen, AUM)

Closing song.

To adapt the prayer for group work, whether in person or remote, ask each participant to interpret one line or section, expanding it with their own meaning. Move through each member of the group to complete the prayer.

There are many spirits that you can contact through prayer. They are waiting to help you, but will rarely do so unless invited. When you invite them to help you, offering your intention and gratitude, you will walk with greater protection.

It is up to every one of us to ask for help from our allies and spirit friends. If you do not know who to ask, or where to direct your request for aid, simply make the call into the white light heart network of infinitely expanding love that exists everywhere, connecting you with yourself and others.

Once this is done, it is of utmost importance that you pay attention to your inner perceptions. Trust that they are real and verify them through listening and responding. We live in physical, emotional, symbolic and spiritual ecologies. Wake up to them and understand yourself as part of them, and stand on your own.

Introduction to ACT

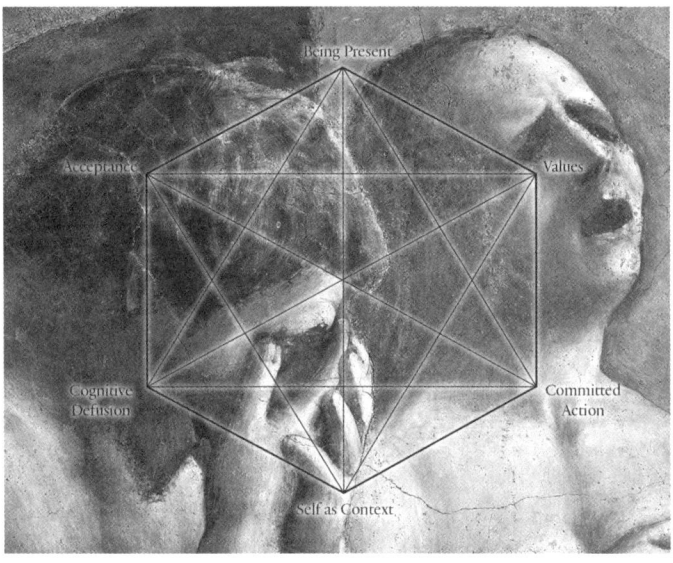

Basic Principles

Acceptance and Commitment Therapy (ACT) is a therapeutic intervention based on behavioural psychology. It is typically used in situations where one may have put areas of their life on hold in response to difficult thoughts or experiences. It maps onto most other psychological, spiritual and political traditions, and is designed to be modified and adapted by those who engage with it. The aim of ACT is to help people cultivate psychological flexibility and commit to action, even in imperfect circumstances.

The term 'acceptance', in this case, means openness to experience, dropping the rope, allowing unpleasant thoughts or feelings to unfold while taking steps to lead a life of vitality and meaning. According to research, the tendency to grapple with thoughts, urges or feelings ultimately increases their negative impact. Instead of challenging distressing thoughts by looking for evidence and coming up with a more rational response, in ACT, the thought is accepted as just a thought, and then defused using a variety of techniques, including mindfulness, metaphors and language.

It is recommended to try the exercises of ACT if you find yourself struggling with avoidance, or if you sense that your thoughts are getting the better of you. Like other forms of behavioural therapy, it is challenging, and requires the completion of aversive exercises. Like many mindfulness-based practices, ACT may not be suitable for everyone; it may be particularly unhelpful if you live with OCD or experience obsessive thinking. As with any self-guided activity, it is always a good idea to check with a practitioner for more advice on whether the practice is suited for your individual needs. If you do wish to explore this practice, let's continue.

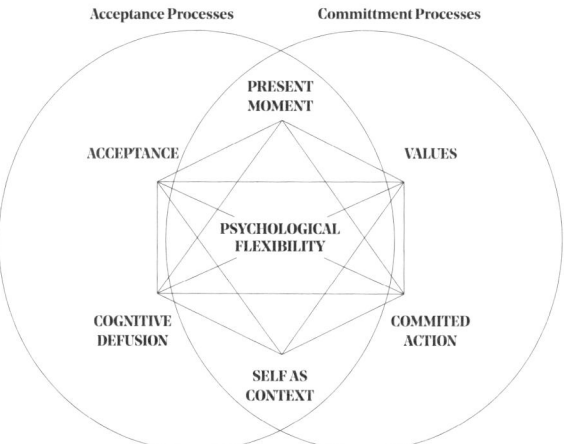

The hexaflex is a key model in ACT. It is a tool with which individuals who practise ACT may orient themselves within the central concepts, allowing them to make behavioural choices more in alignment with their values. It operates as a dynamic engine – as soon as we make changes in one area, the others also begin to shift, creating a sense of movement.

ACT defines destructive cognitive processes as 'psychological inflexibility', organised around six interrelated concepts, listed in the left-hand column below. The ACT approach is part of a wider set of traditions that promote acceptance and action, through encouraging cultivation of 'psychological flexibility', the concepts for which are listed on the right-hand side of the table below.

Psychological Inflexibility	Psychological Flexibility
Cognitive fusion. Seeing mental processes as literally true. An effort to create literal coherence between thoughts, rules, symbols and the external world. Inability to accept contradictions. Attempting to remove, debate or cancel unwanted thoughts.	**Cognitive defusion.** Also 'de-literalisation.' Letting thoughts take a less dominant role, less literal, more paradoxical. Able to let perspective flow, selecting which thoughts to notice and which to let go. Able to operate with a degree of respectful separation from language and images. Able to notice the virtual quality of cognitive processes as an optional collaborator.
Self as content. Identification of self with certain thoughts or behaviours. Adapting behaviour to maintain coherence with this conceptualised self, at the expense of more complex experiences.	**Self as context.** Awareness of self as more than the present moment. "We experience this, but are not defined by this." A sense of the individual as the context within which behaviour may take place. The mind, rather than repeating a fixed story, is able to accept numerous stories. Awareness that all conscious beings are more than their current behaviour. Also known as the 'transcendent self.'
Avoidance. Attempting to remove unwanted experiences or feelings, despite long term costs of doing so. Can include procrastination, addiction, dissociation.	**Acceptance.** Willingness to accept difficult thoughts, feelings and experiences. To turn toward them, as they are. Understanding that the mind's effort to 'avoid unpleasant feelings' inevitably creates more pain in the long term. This is not the same as political acceptance or quietism. In fact, psychological acceptance has been shown to be a formidable political response. It is the willingness to face challenges without seeking to minimise the intensity of perceived threats, realities or feelings.
Conceptualised attention. Lack of awareness of the complexity of the present moment. Frequent past or future conceptualisation. Focus only on certain aspects of the current situation.	**Presence.** Ability to move attention, in the here and now, deliberately, to thoughts, actions, or responses with long term benefits. Noticing the different options available and selecting them, even in difficult or imperfect circumstances. Becoming aware of the rich detail of the present moment.
Separation from values. Alienation. Actions conducted due to social coercion or desire to avoid vulnerability. A struggle to act with love, generosity, care, creativity or other values-based behaviour.	**Values.** Qualities of behaviour conducted in accordance with our personal ideals. These typically are ways of acting that are likely to lead to vulnerability. Values are never completed, do not need to be justified or make sense to the mind. We generally find them in our bodies, at moments of increased vitality. They are culturally idiosyncratic and meaningful to us.
Unworkable action. Taking courses of action that have negative long-term outcomes. This can include impulsive habits as well as excessively rigid, rule-based behaviour.	**Action.** Committing to action. Building consistent habits and rhythms that are aligned with values. Realistic, imperfect and sustainable. Choosing to turn toward experience.

Interestingly, what ACT calls 'psychological flexibility' appears in other traditions, many of which will be familiar to readers. The ability to accept difficult experiences, take action, connect with deep, idiosyncratic values, defuse from judgements and remain present are central to many social movements, spiritual practices and subcultures.

Exercises

The following exercises are brief introductions to ACT in practice.

1. **Misname objects.** Look around the room. Speaking aloud, say the wrong name for all the objects you can see. Call the lamp a dog. Call the ceiling a curtain. Spend enough time on this that your sense of literal meaning is loosened and becomes liquid. This exercise is fun if conducted with others, but is also satisfying alone.

2. **Rewrite the story.** Write out a few hundred words about an experience you find difficult. Something with a history to it. Highlight all thoughts, feelings, memories, sensations, urges, behaviour. Underline every external situation or fact. Now, rewrite the story so the theme, outcome or meaning is totally different, while retaining everything you have underlined and highlighted. The new story needs only to make sense. The purpose is to reveal the way in which our mind creates a fixed narrative when alternatives are available.

3. **Identify values.** Pick a moment in your life where you felt especially betrayed or hurt. A moment after which you went numb. In writing or through memory, ask what this moment suggests about your idiosyncratic passions. What were you trying to do? What kind of person were you trying to be? Allow the answers to sit in your body. Notice if the mind tries to analyse or discourage this investigation.

4. **Do the opposite.** This is a more advanced exercise. Set a timer for 5 or 10 minutes. During this time, do the opposite of what your mind tells you. If your mind tells you not to embrace your friend, do it. You will notice there is a deeper protective mechanism, stopping you from doing anything genuinely dangerous, which operates below the level of conscious thought.

Further reading

If you are curious, there are many exercises available online, as well as books and videos. If you believe you have significant issues with your mental health, there are numerous directories of therapists who are trained in ACT. Remember to shop around. Make sure any professional you decide to pay for is qualified to help with your specific situation and cultural background.

Healing Plants for a Healing Spring
by Paige Emery

What does healing with plants look like within a Western capitalist society? One that infiltrates the interior self and creates external barriers, disabling access to relationships with both the ecology of our bodies and the ecology of plants? To be receptive to plants, we have to soften walls within ourselves. Through sensuous awareness, we can pave the way to forms of healing and communication we might not have previously been comfortable with. Being in tune with our bodies, and the landscapes we inhabit, has been our prevalent mode of existence since the beginning of human time. But opening up to relationships with plants does not have to mean regression. It means finding new ways to coexist in these exponentially changing times.

    Building relationships with plants is an ongoing conversation; express that you are grateful for their presence and you are open and receptive to their healing and guidance. Meet them halfway so they can meet you.

Mint
(Menthe)

In Greek mythology, Menthe was a nymph and lover of Hades, who was turned into a plant by his jealous wife, resulting in a metamorphosed beauty. Mint is ruled by Mercury, and is used medicinally as a cleansing aid for digestion. Peppermint (*mentha x piperita*, a hybrid of watermint and spearmint) is rejuvenating for the mind, promoting a motivating mental alertness and combating mental fatigue.

Ritual: Inhale the scent of peppermint, rub some into your temples, drink mint tea. Take pen to paper without premeditation, allowing your subconscious to stream freely with Mercury at your pen. After your swirling thoughts are released, write down anything you feel compelled to communicate outside of yourself, whether to another person or the world. There is something inside that needs to be said. Shape the paper with words of power. Read this over and realise which words are energising, making you feel alive and driven. Focus on these and let them infuse your body with vivacity, blowing forth your motivation and communication throughout the day.

Violet
(Viola)

Violet is a watery, Venusian plant, aiding the heart and cleansing throughout the body's systems. Tricolour violet (*viola tricolor*) is known as 'heartsease', and has an old tradition of being prescribed for an emotionally upset heart. Violet can also benefit the heart physically; sweet violet (*viola orodata*) can assist blood circulation, which is preventative of heart attacks and strokes. Her fluidity also relieves congestion, dissolves swollen lymph glands and cysts, and soothes the throat and coughs.

Ritual: Hold violets to your heart and ask what needs softening. Take a deep breath, and with the exhale, imagine this swelling area of your life becoming tender. Keep the petals and leaves in your pocket. When heartache or anger comes up, or when you just need some extra love, again with a gentle exhale, extend the softening. In the evening, put the violets in the far right corner of your room next to a bowl of water, offering a prayer of gratitude for the love in your life.

Rosemary
(Salvia rosmarinus)

Fiery rosemary can clear, circulate and protect. His memory-boosting effects have been used since Ancient Greece when students and scholars would place rosemary sprigs in their hair to study. More recent research has shown his ability to stimulate circulation in the head while protecting the mind from mental fatigue and forgetfulness. Delightful for infusing olive oil (but make sure the herb is completely dried, or infuse hot, in order to avoid botulism).

Ritual: Burn a sprig of dried rosemary. Exhale and imagine the internal clearing out of any stagnancies and negativities. Repeat until they are gone. Rub rosemary into your temples, inhale his uplifting aroma and gather your attention in between your eyebrows. Anchor your focus with the vigor of fire, which does not let distractions get in the way. Put a sprig of rosemary in your ear, you can remember what you need, you can be memorable in the way you want to be. This spark and brilliance is already inside you, pave a way for it to come through.

Chamomile
(Matricaria chamomilla)

In Ancient Egypt, chamomile was sacred to the Sun god Ra. The flowers are still planted on graves throughout Eastern Europe to ease the passing of souls to the next realm. Gentle chamomile is a nervine and a relaxant, bringing the nervous system to the parasympathetic state which calms the body. Many studies have shown how this cheerful flower is beneficial for dealing with both anxiety and depression. His calming effects extend throughout the body, as he can aid with digestion, inflammation and sleep.

The relaxed state is a realm where healing can take place. Rather than resisting anxieties and stressors, like the pulling of a rubber band, be so light that you slip through their grip.

Ritual: Make tea from chamomile flowers. First inhale the sunny aroma, then let the warm drink bathe the insides of your mouth for a moment before swallowing. Exhale a heavy, audible sigh. Do this three times. In your following exhale, feel the melting of your shoulders. Move through your body with exhales – melting your chest, your arms, your hands, your stomach, your pelvis, your legs, your feet, until your whole body is in such a relaxed state that you feel as light as a cloud.
This is especially kind to do before bed if you have trouble sleeping, for the anxieties you do not release from the day can follow you into slumber.

Sage
(Salvia officinalis)

Sage, meaning 'wise', and salvia meaning 'to heal' or 'to save'. Sage can both boost cognitive health and support areas of chronic illness (such as asthma, arthritis and colitis) with anti-inflammatory rosmarinic acid. Common sage can add warmth and comfort to any dish and is great for cleansing a space. Use it in substitute for white sage in the US, which is sacred to some Indigenous communities and at risk from being over-harvested.

Ritual: Burn dried common sage and wave the smoke to encompass every part of your body, asking it to cleanse out any blockages in your mind and body. Steep the soft leaves in a tea and call upon wisdom and emotional strength as you slowly sip, breathing into the space between your eyebrows.

Rose
(Rosa)

Well known for love and beauty throughout the ages, roses have been called the 'Queen of Flowers' since the second century and were used by Cleopatra in beauty balms and seductive room adornments. Rose therapeutically promotes love and beauty as well, her aroma uplifting the mood and her anti-aging effects boosting skin health for a glowing complexion.

Rituals: Hold rose in your hand and put it on your heart. Put your other hand on top, look in the mirror and say, with brutal honesty, "I love you." Do this three times, the first thing in the morning, every morning. Aestheticise the mundane in your sanctuary with Taurus.

Indulge in a bath sensualised with rose petals. Sprinkle rose in tea, chocolate, pancakes, make them opulent. Place roses in the far right corner of your bedroom, write a love letter to yourself with a pen of Eros, telling all the unique things you love about yourself and are proud of.

Dandelion
(Taraxacum)

Known as the 'rustic oracle' in the language of flowers, dandelion is a humbly beneficial plant that should not be weeded away. Medicinally, he is revered for cleansing and protecting the liver, an organ with critical roles that include regulating energy, hormones, and chemical levels in the blood. Dandelion also does wonders for the earth, as he helps facilitate healthy soil and promotes nutrient availability to the neighbouring plants. Stop the toxic weed killers, and instead put dandelion leaves and flowers in a salad, the flowers and roots in a tea.

Ritual: Hold a dandelion head and focus on intentions of growth. Ask your spirit guides for extra strength and inspiration to propel you forward. As you blow the wisping seeds, visualise your intentions coming into being.

Clover
(Trifolium repens)

The Celtic Druids saw clover as a bearer of good luck, his three leaves a symbol of earth, sky and water, long before he became Ireland's national flower. Hildegard of Bingen prescribed him as an eye wash, to take fogginess out of the eyes. Native Americans have long used him for coughs, colds and fevers. Clover is also an eco-friendly alternative to grass lawns, and environmentally beneficial as a cover crop.

Ritual: Acquire a green candle (white will also do) and cleanse it. Rub oil into the top (olive oil will do) to create an adhesive surface, then press clover pieces into the oil while focusing on an intention you want to come true. Light the candle while visualising your intention as a vivid reality.

Sanctifying Our Home Spaces
by Leila Sadeghee

The word 'sacred' connotes a sense of elevation from everyday life, of preserving or reserving time, energy and presence in a special way. There's also the awareness that there is something higher or more refined at stake – something that needs protection or attention, lest it be sullied or undone. Sacred is the opposite of mundane, which suggests that it is not boring or dull.

I use the phrase 'transactional reality' to refer to the mundane, because, for me, the sacred is actually not separate from the 'worldliness of the world', but rather, is the deeper aspect of all dimensions of life. 'Transactional' refers, in this sense, to the layer of experience where the sacred is forgotten or unacknowledged – where personal accomplishment and comfort are being celebrated without a sense of being linked to anything higher.

I think it's fair to say that I have dedicated my life to celebrating the sacred and making it more apparent, accessible and enjoyable in my work, in my relationships and in my home.

Sacredness moves in the hush of beauty and reverence. Connecting to sacredness helps you to get a bigger perspective and remember what's really important to you. It's about honouring the best in life and opening up our capacity to let go of what is not important. The more you connect to sacredness, the more beauty you see around you, and the easier it is to keep a loving perspective throughout life's challenges. Sacredness is all about love, and making your home more sacred is an act of bringing more love into your whole life.

Your home is sacred, whether you treat it as such or not; same as your body, your breath, and your choices. What are your ways of bringing the sacred forward in your life?

It wasn't until I was an adult that I made my first altar, which was related to spiritual practice and cultivating sacredness in my life. I was living at the Omega Institute for Holistic Studies in Rhinebeck, New York, and was very inspired by the incredible florist artist, Anthony Flowers Ward, who created arrangements of flowers and found objects, which he would leave in the most unexpected places all over campus. Whenever I stumbled upon one of his pieces tucked between a pair of rocks on the path up to my room, I would be instantly reminded to pay attention, to cherish and to wake up to beauty.

At the time I couldn't afford to take his class on flower artistry, so I took matters into my own hands. On my daily three-hour walk around the lake, I gathered twigs, weeds and wildflowers. I collected vases from the local charity shop. I studied and emulated his work, crafting weird and wonderful forms for my own delight. In my tiny cabin room, I constructed my first formal altar: a wildflower explosion at the foot of my bed, an altar dedicated to my love of the natural world, to my healing, to beauty – and most of all to my own creative process. This altar was a symbolic articulation of my highest aspirations, even though I didn't know it at the time.

Since those early days of my practice, I have lived in homes where I made an altar and ones where I did not. The difference in the kind of things that happened in my life with and without altars is pretty much day to night. In my last few flats, I specifically sought a space where the altar could be the focal point of the room. I want my attention to be organised towards the sacred. I have learned how easy it is for my attention to move towards something else, despite my years of practice.

The following are some guidelines for bringing more sacredness to your home.

Curiosity

What is the space of your home dedicated to? What features have pride of place in your living room – in the other rooms? What are those features connected to? What kinds of energies enter your home through them? A plant is a very different feature than a television. Notice what is present and how these features contribute to the space.

Consider what version of yourself – past, present or envisaged future – this space makes sense for. Consider ways that the person you are becoming may need some elements to be added or removed.

Sense

Make a perimeter walk around your home. Stand in corners and feel the energy that is present there. Notice the view of the space from the corners. Make note of any impulses to make changes or flashes of insight that occur with this walk. You might set your perimeter walk to music with a track featuring theta wave binaural beats.

Intend

Clarify your intention around bringing more sacredness into your home. Journal or contemplate this intention as you prepare to take action.

Cleanse

Have a spring clean or declutter. Add or remove items that reflect the self you are becoming.

Then, do an elemental energy purification. Walk counterclockwise around the perimeter four times, each iteration for an element, holding the intention to cleanse the transactional and stagnant energies from your home. (It's not that the transactional is bad, it's just that you want to clear the way for more sacredness and the charge of love).

For air, take a bell and ring it as you walk, or use dried herbs for smudging (locally grown or wild sourced are best). Pause at any points where you feel you want to have more of an impact.

For fire, walk with a candle, pausing in the corners. Take your hand and pass it over the flame, gesturing for the flame to cleanse the perimeter.

For water, bless some water or use water gathered from a sacred spring or well. Sprinkle it with your fingers along the way. Pause in the corners.

For earth, sprinkle salt (minimally or unprocessed) along the perimeter during your walk, pausing in the corners. Ideally do not vacuum, but use your hand to pick it up and dispose of it in nature. If you have to vacuum, wait a bit before you do it.

Build

Build an altar. Dedicate a space to sanctity in your home. Bring to it what is most sacred and celebrated in your heart. You can also place altars in each room of your home to bring particular healing frequencies to each space. Honour the divine, honour nature, honour ancestors – make a physical honouring space for the sacred.

Bless

What blessing do you want to bring to your home? Craft a song, or a piece of writing that is a heartfelt blessing for your place. Using your own voice to sing or say your blessings is so powerful. A found blessing or invocation that someone else has written is also perfect. Make another perimeter walk, this time clockwise, holding your sacred intention.

Bless your home each time you enter and exit. Mark your intention to bless your home with a sign on your door, or an object to remind you.

Explore

Spend time on deepening the value of the sacred. Meditate and spend time at your altar. Keep attuning and updating your space to who you are and who you are becoming.

Celebrate the sacred in all you do, Blessed One!

Semi-Wilderness: A Guide to Seed Bombs
by Jenna Sutela

Seed balls, or seed bombs, are an ancient technique for propagating new plants without opening up the soil with cultivation tools, such as a plough. The Japanese 'natural farming' pioneer Masanobu Fukuoka rediscovered seed bombs in 1938, calling them 'earth dumplings'.

The architecture of seed bombs is simple: seeds are combined with clay and compost, the mixture moistened with water and rolled into balls. These are allowed to dry in the sun, then cast out into fields at an appropriate time of the year, depending on the seed mixture and rainfall.

As in bonsai, a practice in which planting a tree off-centre in the pot is believed to make space for the divine, seed bombing allows for what Fukuoka calls 'semi-wilderness'. Nature decides what will grow, where and when germination will occur, be that within the next few days or several seasons away. According to Fukuoka, plants grown in this way become particularly strong.

Seed Bomb Recipe

The following ingredient ratios are taken from Fukuoka's suggestion:

5 parts dry, powdered clay (preferably red)
3 parts dry, fine sifted organic compost
1 part seeds
1–2 parts water (to moisten as needed)

Beyond this basic recipe, it's possible to add other elements depending on your circumstances and desired outcomes. For example, a portion of fibres – such as paper mash with love letters or sigils to be charged by the soil – can be added to give the seed bombs greater tensile and spiritual strength.

Innoculating the bombs with native forest soil invites populations of diverse fungi along for the flight, to support woody perennial development. Natural farming, after Fukuoka, is based on recognising the complexity of living organisms that shape the ecosystem, while putting it to use in a symbiotic, spontaneous way.

For further reading see Masanobu Fukuoka, *Sowing Seeds in the Desert: Natural Farming, Global Restoration, and Ultimate Food Security*, Chelsea Green, 2012.

Kriyas for the Equinox and Solstice
by Rachel Okimo

The word *kriya*, meaning 'completed action', refers to a technology found within many yogic traditions. Kriya practices use a combination of postures, breath, sound and meditation techniques to produce specific states of being. There are thousands of kriyas within the system of kriya yoga, and each one affects the body, mind and spirit in a unique and specialised way. Practising kriyas can produce physical and mental changes that allow the practitioner to access deeper states of mindfulness, harmony and expansion. Done every day (many of the practices are short and sweet) kriyas can help transform our physical and mental agility as well as our emotional wellbeing.

The key to practising kriya is in the meaning. We must complete the specific tasks and times for the kriya to be 'complete' and therefore receive the benefits to our system. As one of the kriya yoga masters says: "Keep up and you will be kept up!"

Practices for Equinoxes

The equinox refers to the time in the calendar when daylight and nighttime are of approximately equal duration. Perfect kriya practices to enhance this beautiful time of the year are those that complement the balancing energy that the equinoxes bring.

For the Spring Equinox
Tattva Balance: Beyond Stress and Duality (3 minutes)

A powerful kriya that brings clarity to the mind, equanimity between the right and left hemispheres of the brain and balance to the five elemental forces within the energetic body.

Practise for three minutes every day for forty days through the month of March, to bring clarity and balance for working with equinox energy, to manifest new endeavours or refresh current ones in this time of beginnings, potential and possibility.

1. Sit comfortably on the floor or chair. Apply a light Jalandhara Bandha (throat lock).
2. Raise the arms with the elbows bent until the hands meet at the level of the heart, in front of the chest. The forearms make a straight line, parallel to the ground.
3. Spread the fingers of both hands. Touch the fingertips and thumb tips of opposite hands together. Create enough pressure to join the first segments of each finger. Stretch the thumbs back and point toward the torso. The fingers are bent slightly due to the pressure. The palms are separated.
4. Fix your eyes at the tip of the nose.
5. Create the following breathing pattern: inhale smoothly and deeply through the nose. Exhale through the rounded lips in eight equal, emphatic strokes. On each exhale, pull the navel point in sharply. Continue for three minutes.
6. To end: inhale deeply, hold for 10-30 seconds, and exhale. Inhale again and shake the hands. Relax.

For the Autumn Equinox
Kirtan Kriya

A powerful kriya that brings clarity to the mind, equanimity between the right and left hemispheres of the brain and balance to the five elemental forces within the energetic body.

Practise for three minutes every day for forty days through the month of March, to bring clarity and balance for working with equinox energy, to manifest new endeavours or refresh current ones in this time of beginnings, potential and possibility.

This kriya represents the culmination or completion of a cycle. The seed mantras represent the natural cycles of birth (Saa) life (Taa) death (Naa) and rebirth (Maa). The same cycles present in all creation – from abstract forms such as thoughts and feelings to material endeavours such as our projects.

This kriya is very potent for the completion of cycles and moving through old patterns and habits during this season of change. Repeating the combination of four *mudras*, linked to four primal sounds clears the subconscious mind, creates mental balance and enables deep healing. The four sounds SaaTaa Naa Maa, deriving from the Gurmukhi seed mantra Sat Nam, meaning 'true essence', represent birth, life, death, and rebirth. This is the cycle of creation. First chant out loud (the human voice), then chant with a strong whisper (the voice of lovers), then mentally vibrate the mantra (the divine voice). To complete Kirtan kriya you reverse the sequence, continuing silent with chanting, then whispering, then chanting out loud.

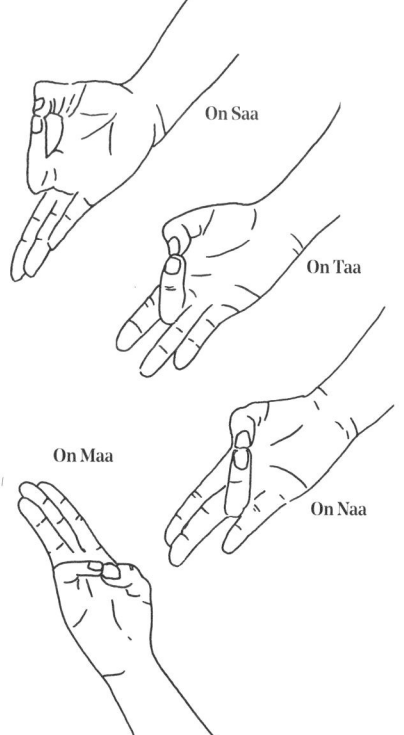

On Saa

On Taa

On Maa

On Naa

Chanting Aloud (5 minutes)

1. Sit in a comfortable seat on the floor or in a chair with a light Jalandhara Bandha (throat lock).
2. Wrists on the knees, arms and elbows straight, start with hands in Gyan Mudra (index finger touching thumb).
3. Meditate at the brow point.
4. Chant "Saa, Taa, Naa, Maa" in full voice.
5. With each sound, alternate through four mudras, touching each finger in turn to the thumb:
   - On Saa, touch the first (Jupiter) finger
   - On Taa, touch the second (Saturn) finger
   - On Naa, touch the third (Sun) finger
   - On Maa, touch the fourth (Mercury) finger
6. As you chant, imagine the energy of each sound moving down through the crown chakra, and then out through the middle brow point (ajna chakra) into space itself.

Whisper (5 minutes)

Continue the sequence while chanting in a strong whisper.

Vibrate Silently (10 minutes)
Continue the sequence while chanting silently, mentally vibrating the mantra.

Whisper (5 minutes)
Continue the sequence while chanting with a strong whisper.

Chanting Aloud (5 minutes)
Continue the sequence while chanting out loud.

Finishing (1 minute)
Inhale deeply and suspend the breath as long as comfortable for up to a minute. Relax the breath smoothly to complete at least one minute of absolute stillness and silence. Then, stretch the hands up as far as possible and spread the fingers wide. Stretch the spine and take several deep breaths. Relax.

Eye Focus: Brow point
Mantra: Saa, Taa, Naa, Maa

Practices For the Solstices

Solstices suggest a peak or an extreme. The lightest and the darkest moments of the year represent the lightest and darkest moments within us.

For the Summer Solstice
Trataka Meditation

Light can manifest as exuberance, energy, lightheartedness, motivation. Practising at its peak allows us to be supported with the natural extra energy that is being beamed at us on the longest day of the year. A beautiful practice any time of the year but especially at the summer solstice is *trataka*, a simple meditation that connects us to the power of light, improves concentration and vision and has a purifying and invigorating effect. Trataka is a gazing practice that can direct attention on a symbol or *yantra*. A popular form is candle gazing: when looking at the flame, work on the capacity to see the flame and its light without hallucinating any images within the flame. Meditate on that radiance for 15-31 minutes, with as little blinking as possible.

1. Find a quiet environment.
2. Sit in a comfortable position on the floor or a chair.
3. Position a candle about seven feet away.
4. Focus your eyes on the flame and see the corona of light around the flame. See the area just under the hottest tip of the flame where there is a dark spot; both light and dark coexist at this point. Meditate on this.
5. Concentrate at the middle brow point. This will stimulate the frontal lobes of the brain. Blink as little as possible.
6. To end, inhale deeply, close the eyelids, and put the image of the radiant light at the brow point of concentration.

For the Winter Solstice
The Inner Sun: Immune System Booster

The winter solstice is a time when the fewest of the sun's rays are available. As the sun is the energy and light giver: when there is less available to us, we must draw from our own inner light to support and nourish ourselves. A powerful practice for sustaining our energy levels, immune system and hormonal balance is this kriya, which stimulates *agni* (internal heat) in order to galvanise the nervous system and the brain. Begin with three minutes, and with gradual practice you can extend the practice to 31 minutes.

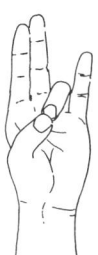

Surya Mudra

1. Sit comfortably on the floor or in a chair. Find a tall and supported posture. Cover your head for the duration of the practice.
2. Bend the left arm and raise the hand up to shoulder level. The palm faces forward. The forearm is perpendicular to the ground.
3. Make Surya Mudra with the left hand (touch the tip of the ring finger to the tip of the thumb).
4. Make a fist of the right hand, pressing the tip of the fingers into the pads at the base of the fingers; extend the index finger. With the extended index finger, gently close off the right nostril.
5. Concentrate at the middle brow point, the seat of intuition.
6. Begin a steady, powerful Breath of Fire. Inhaling and exhaling quickly and evenly through the nose. Emphasise the beat at the navel; the navel moves rapidly and forcefully.

To End
1. Inhale deeply and hold the breath.
2. Interlace all the fingers (beginning with the right thumb uppermost) and put the palms in front at a level just below the throat and slightly away from the body.
3. Try to pull the fingers apart with force as you resist and create a great tension.
4. Exhale when you need to.
5. Repeat this sequence three more times.
6. On the last exhale, discharge the breath by blowing through your upturned lips, with the tongue curled back on the roof of the mouth.

Guide to Seasonal Fungi
by Ellen Percival

Spring
Scarlet Elf Cup

Sarcoscypha austriaca and
Sarcoscypha coccinea

These bright red cup fungi emerge from decomposing sticks in early spring, their colour popping out from their surroundings. It was long thought that in the UK they were just the one species (*s. coccinea*) but in recent decades it's been found that there are in fact two species, *s. coccinea* and *s. austriaca*. Adding to the intrigue, it seems that *s. austriaca* is in fact the most common of the two, by quite a long way, and that *s. coccinea* is likely to be pretty rare. The two species can't be told apart with the naked eye, which illustrates some of the mystery of fungi as a whole: many species look outwardly identical, and can only be identified through light microscopy, chemical staining or genetic testing. These are sometimes known as cryptic species, due to being hidden 'secretly' in plain sight. With fungi there is always more going on under the surface than you might think, and surrendering to not knowing can be an important first step.

If you come across a scarlet elf cup you can attempt a rough-and-ready field identification using a hand lens (available cheaply on the Internet) or a magnifying glass. *S. coccinea* sometimes has very finely hairy or toothed cup margins, while *s. austriaca* tends to have a blunter, slightly thicker margin. The true test is to have a look under a microscope: the outside of the cup is home to tiny microscopic hairs, which are straight to wavy in *s. coccinea*, and very curly in *s. austriaca*. If you find some scarlet elf cups it doesn't matter if you have a microscope or not, you can still help other mycologists by making a biological record using an app like iRecord. This helps to increase knowledge of where these species are found, and sign-posts the way for future enthusiasts and enquirers. Just make sure to record the fungus as *sarcoscypha sp.* instead of a particular species. You can also collect one or two cups and dry them out at home, making sure they don't get too hot (over 40°C) or go mouldy, and take the specimens to a local fungus group, who will often be happy to help you investigate further. They're also, technically, edible, but why eat them when there's so much more to explore?

Summer
Coral Tooth Fungus

Hericium corralloides

This beautiful and eye-catching fungus can be found from late summer, fruiting from decomposing trunks and branches, particularly of beech, birch and ash trees. As well as being appealing to the eye, it is very rare, and will be a source of great excitement to mycologists if you locate one. Just be careful to keep the location secret and share only with trusted parties, as members of the *hericium* genus are some of the few fungi to be legally protected in the UK and are simultaneously highly prized for their gourmet and medicinal properties, thus some people are keen to hunt them down and consume them. But, do not despair, an increasing number are grown commercially, and this is the most fungus-friendly way to sample them, rather than collecting them from the wild. *Hericium erinaceus*, aka Lion's Mane, is the most famous member of the genus, and the species usually cultivated. For a long time it was thought that members of the *hericium* genus were even less common than they're thought to be today (which is still very rare), however genetic testing of living wood samples tells us that these species occur relatively frequently, passing their time unnoticed inside of trees, and it is their visible fruiting that is truly rare.

Autumn
Liberty Cap

Psilocybe semilanceata

Named after their resemblance to Phrygian caps, which came to represent freedom and liberty in the French Revolution, this iconic species is highly sought after, and likely one of the most foraged. In the UK picking liberty caps is illegal, but quietly admiring them at a distance, of course, is not. I don't encourage or condone illegal activity, but if you're going to engage in it, it's better to do so safely. The key is not to confuse *p. semilanceata* with other species that look alike, which may cause gastrointestinal distress if eaten. If in doubt it's best to ask someone with a trusted and experienced eye, as these species can be tricky to distinguish without a bit of practice. This process is known amongst naturalists as "getting your eye in" or having a grasp on the "jizz" of a species (I kid you not). Members of the genus *mycena* are often confused with this species, and if you're in a dung-rich habitat *protostropharia semiglobata* can add confusion to the mix. Looking these up in a field guide or online is a good place to start familiarising yourself with similar-looking species. Liberty caps can be seen from as early as mid-August to as late as January, depending on the year. Although they seem to have a preference for grazed, unfertilised grassland they can be found in a wide range of grassy habitats, including high-maintenance lawns and even dry ski slopes. Their spores are melanised, meaning they are protected by an outer coating of melanin, the same molecule responsible for human skin colour. This is thought to allow them to pass safely through the guts of grazing animals.

Winter
Wavy Cup

Psilocybe cyanescens

Another highly sought-after species, typically found later in the season than its smaller and more delicately-formed cousin, the liberty cap. Unlike liberty caps, which are only found in grassland, wavy caps are a wood-loving species, and are often found fruiting in clusters on ornamental chipped wood. (A 2004 study noted that they were significantly less keen on chipped bark.) Again, care should be taken when identifying these, and they are subject to the same legal constraints as liberty caps. Admiration from afar is all that is allowed. Species not to confuse them with include *leratiomyces ceres* (the redlead roundhead) in particular, which often grows alongside *p. cyanescens* and is poisonous. Redlead roundheads have a distinctively red cap, the edges of which are not 'wavy'. Nor do their stems bruise blue. Their spores, however, are roughly the same colour, and overall the species do broadly resemble each other. This is an instance where if you are in even the smallest bit of doubt about a discovery you should seek advice. Other commonly co-occurring species from the same woodchip habitat include *psathyrella microrhiza, leratiomyces percevalii, agrocybe putaminum* and *gymnopus biformis*.

Spellcraft
by Bones Tan Jones

there are many ways to spell magic. there are many tools to build ritual. there are gardens of plants with which we can honour the planets. there are ten thousand ways to hold space for our highest intentions. a spell can be a poem read in the mirror, or those extra spices sprinkled on your food. you can spell with the wind as rose petals fall from your hands, and you can cast spells with your desires as you plunge deep into earth's lakes. a spell is waking up in the morning awakening your lungs to the new dawn, stretching your muscles and feeling them filled with the potential of the day ahead. sitting with a tree and calling them cousins, feeling their roots below ground you – while the spells of clouds and sun above kiss your face with their offerings. spelling your name is an incantation of belonging, being called our correct pronouns is a spell of visibility. learn the names of the herbs and their bountiful uses, and use them as allies in this journey. spell the planets and their powers and we will find kin within the stars.

engage in this ritual of intent with all you do, and magic will spell its way into your life with ease.

When beginning a spell, it is important to be clear with your intention, with what you desire to manifest. Hold reverence for the universal powers working in your favour. What we put out into the world, we receive back threefold: this is the basics of spellcraft. By creating a ritual around our intention and powering it with the magic of herbs, the alignments of the planets and the weaving of words, we are opening ourselves up to receive the blessings of the universe.

Casting a spell is a powerful act of owning your desires and taking control of your destiny, but it must also be an act of respect for all beings, therefore the only lore in witchcraft is "if it harm none, do what thou wilt". Always use your power for the greatest good of all concerned, and never use magic to manipulate others. I believe that all of us have the power within us to manifest our desires, so awaken your inner magic and start manifesting what you deserve! We all have the tools around us to create a spell; I don't believe in spending money on 'witchy' supplies just to make a spell. However, becoming friends with the plants that grow around us, learning their uses and their planetary alignments helps us connect with the larger web of the universe. Making things such as herbal incenses, herb baths, teas and tinctures are all very powerful ways to work with herbal energy.

Planets and Their Energies

Herbs of the **Sun** are perfect for all rituals of friendship, healing, divine power and bringing more brightness into your life. **Moon**-ruled herbs invoke clairvoyance, dream connection and oceanic rites into your magic. The planet of **Mars** rules conflict, courage, competition, physical strength and lust; using herbs ruled by Mars herbs in your magic can aid with these matters. Herbs of **Mercury**, the planet of communication, can be used in spells for swift communicating, as well as help with studying, mind matters or divination. When manifesting wealth and luck into your life, **Jupiter**-ruled herbs would be best. When creating a spell to bring in self-love, pleasure, art or music, use herbs ruled by the passionate planet of **Venus**. **Saturn**, the planet of death and rebirth, brings structure and meaning to our world. Spells concerning these matters, as well as destroying diseases, pests, terminations of any kind and aligning with the cycle of life, should bring in Saturn-ruled herbs.

Days of the week also have their own potencies:
Sunday - ruled by the Sun
Monday - ruled by the Moon
Tuesday - ruled by Mars
Wednesday - ruled by Mercury
Thursday - ruled by Jupiter
Friday - ruled by Venus
Saturday - ruled by Saturn

Once you have set your intentions and done your ritual, the magic does not end. It is important to continue to do the work on ourselves in our everyday lives to heighten our awareness of this magic, and deepen our understanding of our rhythms. Keeping a spellbook, often called a Book of Shadows, to keep track of your spellwork is an important practice, as well as journaling in your daily life. Create your own daily set of practices that work for you.

Simple Manifestation Spell

Ruled by the Sun, with the elemental energies of fire and in the astrological sign of Leo, the simple bay leaf can be a great friend, not only for smoke cleansing, but for spellcraft.

Sit with your intention, feel what it feels to already live it as your truth. Light a candle. Write your intention onto the bay leaf, clear and simple, using only positive words. Burn the bay leaf, watching the leaf crackle as the flame devours your intention, turning it into smoke curling up into the atmosphere. Meditate on this. Your truth is already within you, it is already waiting for you. In ritual spellcraft, we add power to our intentions through aligning with our plant and planetary allies. Our higher selves acknowledge our desires and alert the universe that we are ready to receive these blessings, for the greater good of all concerned.

Weather Watching
by Jay Drinkall

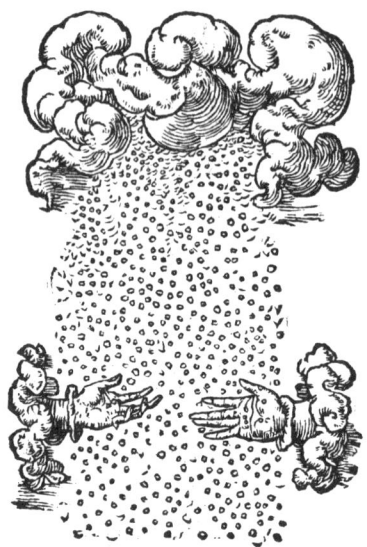

Image: 'Non quae super terram', illustration in Claude Paradin's Devises Heroïques, 1557.

'We are not masters of the climate, nor are we just spatially 'in' it. As weather-bodies, we are thick with climatic intra-actions; we are makers of climate-time. Together we are weathering the world.'
– Astrida Niemanis & Rachel Loewen Walker

All weather is ultimately caused by the sun. The sun's heat warms air differently across Earth, and as warm pockets rise, cold air rushes in from underneath to replace the hotter, less dense air. Water is carried up to higher, colder levels of the atmosphere as vapour, and hurls itself back to Earth as rain or snow when it hits low temperatures. Weather conditions that we may commonly experience include wind, cloud, rain, snow, fog and dust storms. Rarer events include natural disasters like tornadoes, floods, hurricanes, typhoons and ice storms. Almost all familiar weather phenomena occur in the troposphere – the lower part of the atmosphere, which contains 99% of the Earth's atmospheric water vapour and which we also inhabit. Changes in weather are often caused by 'fronts' – boundaries between warring air masses – that produce contrasting weather conditions. Fronts may be defined as 'strong' or 'weak': the higher the contrast (say, between a very warm, moist air mass and a cool and dry one), the higher the drama.

Weather is also something else. It's part of the intimate vernacular of our local environment: our most mundane and pervasive connection to the earth, manifesting in our small talk and influencing the way we meet one another, in our shared need for shelter or orientation toward sunlight. Conversations about the weather are a common kind of lay prophecy; one type of weather can often herald the next. While national and regional meteorological forecasting relies on the sequencing of large trends, weather as we physically encounter it – 'micro-weather' – can be unruly and unpredictable, with immediate forecasts better made through the senses. Weather is the day-to-day experience of our environment, local but not parochial: weather knowledge is something you can carry with you.

In this moment of drastic and unsettling disruption to our weather and climate, I have found solace in developing a regular practice of weather observation. Rather than just an abstract phenomenon that happens to us, the weather is part of us and we're part of it. We are both subject to the weather and complicit in altering the climate. Feeling and acknowledging this ambiguous relationship can give a sense of embodiment and presence that I have found grounding in moments of climate anxiety, as anxiety tends to be future-oriented. By inhabiting weather-moments, we can round out the sense of ecological grief that many of us feel, through the act of witnessing.

Observing the Weather

- Take time to go outside each day, and observe what you see. Keep a weather notebook for this purpose, or incorporate the reflections into any existing journal for nature-based activities.
- Until you have finished estimating the weather with your senses, resist the temptation to check the weather on your phone, or look at the barometer or thermometer. How warm or cold does it feel? Record your predictions and their results.
- What shape are the clouds today? How high are they? What type do you think they could be? How fast are they moving? How much light is visible?
- How is the light changing, hour-by-hour?
- Is there any wind? Is it blustery or smooth? Does it seem steady or undecided about its direction?
- Is there any rain today? Did you expect it? Do you think there will be any later, based on the movement of the clouds, wind and light levels?
- Through building an observational practice over time, you will become attuned to small causes and effects of weather, and be able to predict basic changes through your senses.

Common Types of Cloud

There are many types of weather, many of which are location-specific. Clouds, however, are widespread, and can be a great foundation for building a practice of weather watching.

Note: the following are really cloud *groups*, as several subtypes can be found within each category, including rare and fabulous formations such as noctilucent and lenticular, which require special conditions in order to form.

- Cumulus – from *cumulo*, 'heaped'. One of the most common types of cloud. Individual forms are puffy, piled up like marshmallows, perhaps flat on the bottom as though resting on a pane of glass. Think of a child's drawing. The tops of these clouds are mostly brilliant white tufts when lit by the sun. Indicates: fair weather; cumulus are often present on bright, sunny days. However, if conditions allow, cumulus can grow into towering cumulus congestus or cumulonimbus, which can produce showers. Generally, if a cumulus cloud is taller than it is wide, it can produce rain.

- Stratus – 'layered', 'flattened' or 'spread out'. These clouds tend to be low, flat and featureless, occluding the sky in a blanket of white or grey. The lowest-lying cloud, these sometimes form from fog or mist. Dull days under a thick blanket of 'nebulosus' stratus can be very dark if the cloud is thick enough, or curiously bright under thinner layers. The semi-lit atmosphere they produce can feel a little like existing inside a ping-pong ball. These clouds can persist for long periods of time, as they form in calm, stable conditions when gentle breezes raise cool, moist air over colder land or ocean surfaces. Indicates: a heavy-feeling atmosphere, or drizzle if the cloud is thick enough.

- Nimbostratus – 'rainy' + 'layered'. These dark, featureless strata of cloud are thick enough to block out the sun and produce persistent rain. Shaped in layers or large areas of individual cells, these clouds are found low in the troposphere and will often appear to cover the whole of the sky. Indicates: continuous rain or snow, until the associated weather front passes over. The presence of hail, thunder or lightning indicates cumulonimbus rather than nimbostratus.

- Cirrus – 'curl' or 'tendril'. These clouds often appear in white, wispy, filamentous, tufted streaks, sometimes called 'mare's tails'. Composed of ice, they are found in the highest layer of the troposphere. They come in many forms including cirrus fibratus (long streamers), cirrus spissatus (dense, high layers) or cirrus floccus (cotton wool appearance). Indicates: usually fair to pleasant weather, with a change occurring within 24 hours. Due to their high altitudes, they are given their shape by high winds. By watching the movement of cirrus clouds you can tell from which direction weather is approaching.

- Cirrocumulus – think of these as 'curled heaps', or perhaps 'heaped tendrils'. Also known as 'mackerel sky', these high-altitude clouds appear as long, rippling rows of small, rounded puffs, which may resemble fish scales. Usually seen in winter, these clouds are made of ice and 'supercooled' water (which stays liquid at temperatures below 0°C). Indicates: possibly fair, but cold weather. In tropical regions, they may foretell an approaching hurricane.

- Cirrostratus – the gossamer layers of these high, transparent clouds are composed of ice crystals, forming a veil that covers large areas of the sky. Because of their height, they may produce interesting light phenomena: rings, spots or arcs of light around the sun or moon, known as 'halos'. These clouds can be so thin that halos are the only indication that a cirrostratus is present. They are often fringed with cirrus clouds, and can form from slowly rising air or contrails. A good way of distinguishing cirrostratus from the similar altostratus clouds is by looking to the ground: are objects casting shadows? If yes, the clouds are cirrostratus. Indicates: change in the next 24 hours. The subtype cirrostratus nebulosus (meaning 'full of vapour, foggy, cloudy, dark') indicates that an incoming warm front may bring persistent rain within a day, or fair weather. Cirrostratus fibratus (meaning 'fibrous') may bring only light drizzle.

- Cumulonimbus – 'heaped' + 'rain'. These dense, vertical thunderclouds can be incredibly dramatic, with deep, dark bases. They're also huge, with bases that can reach several kilometres across. When vertically developed, this largest of all clouds usually extends through all three cloud-bearing regions of the atmosphere, and the top may drift into an anvil-like shape. Forming from water vapour carried upwards by powerful air currents, even the smallest cumulonimbus cloud dominates its neighbours. Indicates: usually heavy rain, snow, hail, lightning or even tornadoes. The anvil usually points in the direction the storm is moving.

- Stratocumulus (also cumulostratus) – think of these as 'flattened heaps' or 'puffy layers': low, large, rounded masses of stratus that appear in groups, lines or waves, varying in colour from bright white to dark grey. These are the most common clouds, recognisable by their well-defined bases and fluctuating shading. Indicates: a change in weather, usually, as they tend to be present near a warm, cold or occluded front. Stratocumulus clouds can actually be present in all types of weather, but despite often being confused for rainclouds, they rarely produce more than a light drizzle.

- Altocumulus – 'high' + 'heaped'. These 'cloudlets' are small mid-level layers or patches, usually in the shape of rounded clumps. There are many varieties of altocumulus, however, meaning they can appear in a range of shapes. Consisting of ice and water, these clouds have a slightly more ethereal quality than the fluffy, low-hanging cumulus. In fact, they more closely resemble cirrocumulus, but can be told apart from them by the presence of shading – cirrocumulus clouds are white and tiny, but altocumulus clouds can be white or grey with shaded sides. Indicates: settled weather, often. Precipitation from these clouds is rare, but even if rain does fall it doesn't reach the ground. This precipitation can be seen in the form of ghostly sheets of virga ('stripe'), where the rain re-evaporates before reaching the Earth's surface.

- Altostratus – 'high' + 'flattened' or 'spread out'. Usually grey or blue, these layered, featureless clouds often cover a large area of sky, and evolve from a gradually thickening veil of cirrostratus. Composed of water and ice, parts can be thin enough to allow some sun through. Indicates: change. Altostratus clouds often form ahead of a warm or occluded front. As the front passes, the altostratus layer deepens and bulks out to become nimbostratus, which produces rain or snow. As a result, seeing it can usually indicate a change in weather is on the way.

Notes